T0319028

Cambridge Elements ≡

Elements in the Philosophy of Religion
edited by
Yujin Nagasawa
University of Birmingham

DEPROVINCIALIZING SCIENCE AND RELIGION

Gregory Dawes
University of Otago, New Zealand

CAMBRIDGE
UNIVERSITY PRESS

CAMBRIDGE
UNIVERSITY PRESS

University Printing House, Cambridge CB2 8BS, United Kingdom

One Liberty Plaza, 20th Floor, New York, NY 10006, USA

477 Williamstown Road, Port Melbourne, VIC 3207, Australia

314–321, 3rd Floor, Plot 3, Splendor Forum, Jasola District Centre,
New Delhi – 110025, India

79 Anson Road, #06–04/06, Singapore 079906

Cambridge University Press is part of the University of Cambridge.

It furthers the University's mission by disseminating knowledge in the pursuit of
education, learning, and research at the highest international levels of excellence.

www.cambridge.org
Information on this title: www.cambridge.org/9781108711784 ,
DOI: 10.1017/9781108612623

First published 2021

A catalogue record for this publication is available from the British Library.

ISBN 978-1-108-71178-4 Paperback
ISSN 2399-5165 (online)
ISSN 2515-9763 (print)

Deprovincializing Science and Religion

Elements in the Philosophy of Religion

DOI: 10.1017/9781108612623
First published online: February 2021

Gregory Dawes
University of Otago, New Zealand

Author for correspondence: Gregory Dawes, gregory.dawes@otago.ac.nz

Abstract: To ask about the relation of science and religion is a fool's errand unless we clarify which science we are discussing, whose religion we are speaking about, and what aspects of each we are comparing. This Element sets the study of science and religion in a global context by examining two ways in which humans have understood the natural world. The first is by reference to observable regularities in the behavior of things; the second is by reference to the work of gods, spirits, and ancestors. Under these headings, this work distinguishes three varieties of science and examines their relation to three kinds of religion along four dimensions: beliefs, goals, organizations, and conceptions of knowledge. It also outlines the emergence of a clear distinction between science and religion and an increase in the autonomy of scientific inquiry. It is these developments that have made conflicts between science and religion possible.

Keywords: Ethnoscience, correlative cosmology, Chinese philosophy, Aristotelian philosophy, mythic thought

ISBNs: 9781108711784 (PB), 9781108612623 (OC)
ISSNs: 2399–5165 (online), 2515–9763 (print)

Contents

1 Introductory Remarks

While preparing this work, I looked up the title *Science and Religion* on the online catalogue of the British Library, said to be the largest in the world in terms of the number of items it contains. My search turned up some 33,467 results. Most were short pieces – articles – but a full 7,201 items were books. A search on Google Scholar returned an even larger number: 86,000 items, books, and articles combined. That's just for the full phrase. Searching by the terms "science" and "religion" in any combination returned 2,900,000 items. So there is a lot of material out there. Why have I added to this plethora of literature? What does this Element have to offer?

What it has to offer is a broader vision of the science and religion debate. Seen from a global perspective, the existing literature appears astonishingly provincial. It deals almost exclusively with *modern* science and the *Christian* religion. The aim of this Element is to widen the discussion. It will talk about modern science and Christianity. In doing so, it will address some familiar questions. It will ask, for instance, about apparent conflicts between science and religion, such as Galileo's conflict with the church or the rejection by some believers of Charles Darwin's theory of evolution. But it will not limit itself to modern science. Neither will it restrict itself to one kind of religion. It will present the relation between modern science and the Christian religion as one instance of a broader phenomenon. That phenomenon has to do with two different ways in which humans have thought about what we call "the natural world."

A first way of thinking about the natural world explains its functioning by reference to a set of principles, which are derived from observations of the way the world regularly operates. ("Why did the stone fall when released from my hand?" "Because all objects fall toward the center of the earth when not otherwise supported.") The other interprets and explains the natural world by reference to what we may call "metapersons" (Sahlins 2017: 92) – gods, spirits, and ancestors – who inhabit a realm inaccessible to ordinary perception and who have qualities and powers human beings lack. ("Why was the city destroyed by an earthquake?" "Because God was punishing its inhabitants.")

In our society, these two ways of thinking about the world go by the terms "science" and "religion." Many societies do not distinguish them so clearly; they may even lack these categories altogether. But even when they lack the categories, they employ both ways of thinking, in varying degrees and in differing ways. All peoples interpret and explain what they see happening around them both by reference to observable regularities (and the principles thought to underlie them) and by reference to powerful metapersons, who can be accessed and influenced by prayer and ritual. It is the relation between these two ways of understanding the world that is the topic of this Element.

1.1 A Question of Terminology

What should I call these two forms of understanding? The customary term "religion" will serve for one of them – the one that invokes powerful and normally invisible metapersons – provided we keep in mind the variety of forms religion takes. For the other – that which refers to observable regularities in the way the world operates – I am tempted to use the term "science," while insisting that it be understood in a broader-than-usual sense. But this usage is likely to give rise to misunderstandings, so widespread and firmly rooted is our modern understanding of the word "science."

Take, for instance, the cosmology that underlies Chinese traditional medicine. This is a set of principles, derived from observations of the way the world regularly operates. It generally eschews talk of invisible and powerful metapersons. But what should we call it? No thinker has done more to alert us to the history of intellectual achievement in China than Joseph Needham (1900–95). When Needham began describing this traditional cosmology, he did so under the heading: "The Fundamental Ideas of Chinese Science" (Needham 1956: 216). In one sense, he was right to do so, for the cosmology in question is functionally equivalent to science (Bodde 1991: 11–12). But the principles by which it operates are so different from those of modern science that the use of the term created some confusion (Peterson 1980: 29). Indeed, Needham himself felt compelled to describe many of the practices involved as "pseudo-sciences" (Needham 1956: 216).

However, the use of the term "pseudo-science" is also unhelpful, since it has proved extraordinarily difficult to distinguish science from pseudoscience. But the differences between Chinese cosmology and modern science need to be respected. Similar remarks could be made about other traditions of inquiry into the natural world. Take, for instance, the tradition established by Aristotle (384–322 BCE), which I shall call "natural philosophy." To call this "science" would not only mislead the reader; it would also invite a premature rejection of Aristotelian thought for not doing what (our) science does. So, what term *can* I use? What word would be broad enough to encompass all traditions of organized reflection about the natural world?

With some hesitation, I have chosen to use the Latin term *scientia* for this broader category of knowledge, while keeping the word "science" for "modern science." (The adjective "scientific," however, I shall continue to use for both.) If only for the sake of symmetry, I am tempted to replace the English word "religion" by the corresponding Latin term *religio*. But I shall (for the most part) resist this temptation. The use of another Latin word seems superfluous and the historical associations of the word *religio*, which originally meant something along the lines of "reverence" or "scrupulousness," would also be misleading.

The word *scientia*, by way of contrast, has helpful historical associations. Pronounced as either *ski-en-tia* or *shi-en-zia* (depending on where you learned Latin), the term was widely used by medieval writers, in a way that was broader than our use of the word "science." *Scientia* referred to any body of systematic knowledge of the principles by which the world operates. The most basic of these principles were known by observation; others could be deduced from them. Thinkers in the Aristotelian tradition developed a particular variety of *scientia*. This sought to explain the behavior of objects by grouping them under categories of beings that shared a common nature. But if we stick to the more fundamental sense of the term *scientia*, we can employ it more broadly. We can use it to refer to any systematic body of knowledge, drawn ultimately from observation, that seeks to identify the principles by which the world operates.

1.2 The Science and Religion Literature

I shall come back to these conceptions of *scientia* and religion shortly. But what I have said allows me to restate the point I made earlier about the existing literature. Most such works are discussions of (modern) science and the Christian religion, rather than of the various forms of *scientia* and religion. They limit themselves to one form of *scientia* and to one form of religion. Many of them have an even narrower focus: they examine what is commonly called the "conflict" or "warfare" thesis. So widespread is this theme that a discussion of it can provide us with a path into the existing literature.

What is the "conflict" or "warfare" thesis? In its strongest form, it would involve one or more of the following claims: (a) that science and religion have always been in conflict, (b) that religious belief hinders scientific progress, and that (c) one cannot consistently accept what science tells us while remaining a believer. Stated in this way, the conflict thesis is something of a straw man. Few, if any, thoughtful authors have defended any of these positions. Views (a) and (b) are commonly attributed to two nineteenth-century writers, namely John William Draper (1875) and Andrew Dickson White (1896). Draper and White do offer repeated examples of (what they take to be) conflicts between science and religion. But neither holds that all forms of religion have been opposed to science, hindering its progress, or that religion and science are incompatible (Dawes 2016: 2–8). For Draper, it is Roman Catholicism that poses a threat to science, particularly when its authorities gain political power. For White, the problem lies not with religion as such, as with a certain kind of dogmatic theology: one that uses biblical authority to oppose scientific theorizing.

There are more recent writers who defend a form of conflict thesis. Notable examples are to be found among the thinkers popularly known as the "new atheists," particularly Richard Dawkins, Sam Harris, and Dan Dennett. All three are scientists, or scientifically oriented philosophers, who use their knowledge of science to argue that it is in conflict with religion. Richard Dawkins, for instance, focuses not merely on the claims made by religions, but also the attitude of mind they encourage. Religion, he believes, is opposed to science insofar as it encourages an uncritical acceptance of what is being proposed for belief (Dawkins 2006: 284). But the new atheists are not alone in defending a conflict thesis. A more nuanced version is found, for instance, in the work of the historian and sociologist, Yves Gingras (2017).

Although a modest form of conflict thesis continues to have its advocates, it has fallen largely out of fashion (De Cruz 2018: sect. 1.3). The first to reject it were historians, who pointed out the oversimplifications and sometimes outright errors found in the works of Draper and White. Key figures among the historians include James Moore (1979), who studied the reception of Darwin's work in the English-speaking world, and John Hedley Brooke (1991), whose writings offer insights into the complexity of the religion and science relation. Noteworthy, too, is the work of Jon H. Roberts on nineteenth-century responses to Darwin in America (1988), Edward Larson on the debates regarding the teaching of evolution (1997, 2003), and Ronald Numbers on twentieth-century creationism (2006).

Some opponents of the conflict thesis have tried to set out alternative views of the relation between science and religion. A pioneer in this respect was Ian Barbour. Barbour begins his discussion with the conflict view, which he attributes to both "scientific materialists" and "biblical literalists," before describing three other ways in which science and religion can be thought to be related: "independence," "dialogue," and "integration" (Barbour 1997: 77–105). A more recent analysis of this kind has been offered by Mikael Stenmark (2004), whose discussion of the "dimensions" of the religion and science relation has helped shape the present work. Many such thinkers are themselves religious or are sympathetic to religion. But not all are. The evolutionary biologist Stephen Jay Gould, for example, was not himself a religious thinker. But he argued for a form of the "independence" view, suggesting that science and religion have "nonoverlapping *magisteria*" (NOMA). (As Roman Catholic readers may know, the term *magisteria* is the plural of the Latin *magisterium*, which means "teaching authority.") Science and religion are independent, on this view, since science deals with matters of fact, while religion deals with matters of value (Gould 2001: 739).

Other opponents of the conflict thesis go further, arguing that science and religion, far from being at odds, actually lend support to one another. In doing so, they follow in the footsteps of Robert Merton (1938), who argued that modern science developed within a particular social and religious context, that of Protestant Christianity. Scholars such as Reijer Hooykaas (1972) and Rodney Stark (2006), for instance, have argue that certain religious beliefs prepared the way for scientific thinking. By making a sharp distinction between God and the world, for instance, Jews and Christians are thought to have freed up that world for scientific inquiry. Other authors argue that science actually lends support to religious belief (Swinburne 2010: 44–61) and enriches our view of the divine (Peacocke 2001).

A final view is worth noting because it involves a reaffirmation of the conflict thesis, but in a way that favors religion rather than science. It is found among those known as "creationists," who reject evolutionary theory. In common with the new atheists, creationists agree that there are conflicts between religion and science. But they hold that the fault lies not on the side of religion, but on the side of science. The science on offer, they argue, is not true science; it is what they sometimes describe as "science falsely so-called" (1 Tim 6:20), which is corrupted by atheistic assumptions. A sophisticated version of this view has been advanced by Alvin Plantinga, who blames conflicts on the "naturalism" of the sciences: their refusal to allow any but natural explanations (Plantinga 2011: 311).

1.3 Which *Scientia*, Whose *Religio*?

So much for the existing literature. What about the present Element? What forms of *scientia* and religion will it study and what topics will it address?

1.3.1 Varieties of Scientia

Let me begin with *scientia*. The quest to understand how the natural world operates is (one may assume) as old as human beings themselves. Indeed, there are some broadly "scientific" principles that we may not need to learn, since we are born knowing them. Even infants seem to have certain expectations about their environment and the behavior of physical objects (Spelke 1998). But whatever our native endowment, we seek to supplement it by observation and reflection. Such observations and reflections are the basis of the various forms of *scientia*.

What about religion? Does it have a similar origin? Did religion also arise from attempts to understand how the world operates? Some early anthropologists suggested it did, arguing that those who first developed belief in gods were primitive scientists. They, too, were trying to explain what they saw happening around them: events such as storms or earthquakes. But instead of explaining these by reference to impersonal powers, operating in predictable ways, they explained them as the work of invisible personal agents: gods, spirits, demons, or ancestors. On this view, spirits are simply "personified causes" (Tylor 1913: 108).

This view is not entirely mistaken, for religious beliefs are sometimes used to explain natural phenomena. But as an account of the origin of religion, it seems implausible. First, it is highly speculative, reading modern attitudes back into the distant past (Evans-Pritchard 1965: 24–7). Second, it overlooks the fact that the founding figures of the major religions – think of Moses, Jesus, Muhammad, the Buddha, or Bahā'ullāh – were not regarded as clever observers of the natural world. They were regarded as individuals who had attained personal enlightenment, were divinely inspired, or were incarnations of a divinity. Yet even if stories about gods were not *created* to explain how the world operates, they can still have an explanatory role. They can still be used to tell us why certain events occurred. To this extent, the aims of *scientia* and religion overlap, as we shall see.

For the moment, however, it is *scientia* with which I am concerned. Can I describe more precisely what I mean by this term? The diversity of the traditions embraced by this term might appear to make a definition impossible. But it is worth making an attempt. So here it is. For the purposes of this study, I shall take a *scientia* to be

> a communal tradition of inquiry whose aim is to create a systematic account
> of the principles governing a set of regularly observable phenomena within
> the natural or human world.

Let me spell that out. First, a *scientia* is a communal tradition, that is to say, a collective enterprise that extends over time. Second, its aim is to create a set of general claims that are related to one another in a systematic manner. Third, those claims have to do with what can be regularly observed: with what happens "always or for the most part" (Aristotle 1925: 304 [1027a21–22]).

While there are many traditions of inquiry that would fall under this definition, the present study will focus on three of them. These are (a) *scientia* as integral cosmology (as found in ancient China), (b) *scientia* as natural philosophy (as found in medieval Europe), and (c) *scientia* as a form of specialized knowledge (modern science). Alongside these three categories of *scientia*, I shall also speak of a fourth category, which I shall call "traditional knowledge." This sometimes goes by other names, such as "local knowledge," "indigenous knowledge," and "ethnoscience." It consists of the beliefs about the natural world that are found within small-scale societies, particularly those lacking literacy.

The first form of *scientia* – what I am calling an "integral" cosmology – is "integral" in the sense of all-embracing. It does not merely describe the principles that govern the universe. It also makes normative claims (claims about how we ought to live) that are based on these principles. It is a "cosmology" in the sense of a systematic account of the entities that make up the world and the principles that govern their behavior (Tambiah 1985: 130). The term "cosmology" is often used today to refer to theories about the origins of the universe. But I am using it more broadly. Cosmologies (as I am using the term) may or may not speak of origins, but they do speak of the principles by which the world operates.

My example of an integral cosmology will be the one that emerged in China during the period of the Warring States (403–221 BCE) and that of the Qin (Ch'in) (221–206 BCE) and former Han (206 BCE–9 CE) dynasties. This is sometimes called a "correlative cosmology" because it posits the existence of mutually dependent relations between different classes of phenomena. By the first century BCE, this cosmology had become the dominant way of viewing the world among Chinese thinkers (Harper 1999: 861) and has remained influential until modern times. Cosmologies of this kind are by no means unique to China. A form of correlative cosmology is also found in the history of European thought, in the systems of correspondence so popular during the Renaissance (Graham 1989: 318). Here, too, the correspondences were thought to have normative significance (Tillyard 1943: 82–91). But the intellectual history of China offers a particularly striking example.

My second variety of *scientia*, namely "natural philosophy," was first developed in ancient Greece, but found its fullest expression in the medieval European and Muslim worlds. This is not an integral cosmology of the kind found in China, for its investigation of the natural world is distinguished from mathematics, metaphysics, and ethics. Yet while natural philosophy was distinguished from these other intellectual tasks, it was not divorced from them. Natural philosophy formed part of a larger enterprise. That larger enterprise included moral inquiry and metaphysics, the latter being a kind of (natural) theology, which spoke about the divine.

A third variety of *scientia* is what we call "science," although I shall often refer to it as "*modern* science." This tradition of inquiry began in the seventeenth century, but took on its present form only with the professionalization of scientific disciplines in the nineteenth century. Modern science is itself a diverse enterprise. It embraces many different forms of inquiry and is practiced in different ways in different contexts (Livingstone 2003: 17). But there are two features of modern science that I shall focus on here. The first is its institutionalization in dedicated scientific organizations. The second is its relative isolation from broader intellectual and ethical concerns.

What about my category of "traditional knowledge," the bodies of belief about the natural world found in small-scale societies? One should not, in my view, refer to these as forms of *scientia*. There are two reasons to avoid the term in this context. The first is that while such bodies of knowledge may appeal to general principles – such as that of a "kinship" relation between all things (Prytz-Johansen 2012: 3) – they do not expound these principles in a systematic fashion. A second reason is that traditional knowledge has distinctive features of its own. Some authors have even suggested that the term "knowledge" fails to capture what is involved, preferring the phrase "indigenous ways of living in nature" (Aikenhead & Ogawa 2007: 553). This reflects the idea that traditional knowledge is a way of "being in the world," not merely a way of understanding it. I shall, however, continue to use the term "knowledge," although my use of the term will embrace both practical (skill-based) knowledge and the knowledge expressed in rituals and narratives.

Even if we do not call traditional knowledge "science," it has something in common with the various forms of *scientia*. It also involves conceptions of the natural world and how it operates. Those conceptions fall into four categories. A first category has to do with the classification of natural objects: how the members of a culture pick out and describe and the features of the nonhuman world, particularly plants and animals. A second category is that of etiological beliefs: stories regarding the origins of humans, animals, and features of the landscape. A third category has to do with the properties of natural objects, such as the healing properties of plants or the kind of inner life experienced by animals. A final category is that of practical knowledge – "knowing how" rather than "knowing that" – which is embodied in the learning of certain skills. Each of these forms of knowledge has a slightly different relation to the religious practices of the societies in which they are found.

1.3.2 Varieties of Religion

What about religion? If it is difficult to come up with a definition of *scientia*, it is even more difficult to come up with a definition of religion. But I shall once again make an attempt. For the purposes of this study, I shall take a religion to be

> a communal tradition of ritual action that seeks to make contact with a hidden realm of metapersons and powers and whose goal is to bring this-worldly and/ or other-worldly benefits to the individuals or community in question.

Again, a few words of explanation may be helpful. First, I am defining religion as a form of *practice* rather than a system of *beliefs*. Most philosophers focus on religious beliefs, which is understandable, given their interests. But many communities engage in religious practices without articulating the assumptions that underlie them. Members of such communities surely have beliefs: there are claims about the gods they hold to be true. But for much of the time these beliefs remain implicit. They are not articulated in the form of creeds (Mbiti 1969: 3, 67).

There is a second feature of religion that is highlighted by my definition. It is that religious practices seek to make contact with an "occult" or hidden realm: a world of metapersons and mysterious forces that parallels the observable world of everyday, practical action. Religious practices seek to make contact with this realm in order to benefit the community or individuals involved. Many religions do have a further goal, which is that of ensuring that their practitioners behave in certain ways. But in order to cast the net as widely as possible, I shall avoid making that a defining feature of religion.

What types of religion shall I discuss in the sections that follow? There are many ways of classifying religions. One can, for instance, distinguish between religions for which belief in a god or gods is essential (such as Islam and Christianity) and those (such as Theravada Buddhism) for which belief in gods is of secondary importance. But the classification I shall use here has a different basis. It has to do with the relation of religious practices to the society in which they are found. Based on this criterion, we can distinguish between (a) "diffused" religions, in which religious practices permeate a society, (b) "institutional" religions, which have a distinctive form of organization, and (c) the "privatized" religion of modern secular societies.

"Diffused" religions are easily overlooked, precisely because they are not embodied in distinct institutions (Yang 1961: 20). In a society whose religion is of this kind, people will be aware of the difference between religious and nonreligious practices. They will be aware, for example, of the difference between digging a garden and invoking a god to ensure the plants grow. But the two kinds of activity will be carried out alongside one another, commonly in the same place, at (more or less) the same time, and often by the same practitioners.

Diffused religions can take two forms. There are the diffused religions of small-scale societies. These societies are relatively egalitarian, with little or no social stratification and relatively little specialization of roles. They commonly lack literacy and have simple forms of technology (although the use of their technology may require high levels of skill). In small-scale societies, the community of religious practitioners will be coextensive with some "natural" grouping, such as that of the family or the tribe (Wach 1947: 56–9). But forms of diffused religion are also found in larger, more differentiated societies (such as that of ancient China). What makes a religion a diffused religion in this context is that it is embedded in institutions it has not itself created. In ancient Chinese society, for instance, the veneration of ancestors and local deities did not give rise to distinct community, comparable to the Christian church or the *ummat al-*

islām (the people of Islam). Rather, such religious practices formed an integral part of community life (Yang 1961: 296–8).

So much for diffused religion. A second variety of religion is what I shall call "institutionalized" religion. Religions of this kind have created their own forms of community life. They have systematized and coordinated bodies of beliefs, organized forms of worship, and an established form of leadership (Yang 1961: 294). As in the case of diffused religions, people generally belong to an institutional religion by virtue of being born into a particular family. But the family will be identified as, for instance, a "Christian," a "Muslim," or a "Buddhist" one. In premodern societies, movement from one religious community to another may be possible, but will be rare and socially fraught.

Institutional religions are also of two kinds. There are those that play a dominant role in their societies. Their leaders seek to shape the practices of their society in ways that go beyond the influence exerted on individuals. (The medieval Christian church was an institutional religion of this kind.) Such societies tend towards the "hierocratic," in the sense of being controlled by a religious hierarchy. But there are also institutional religions existing within hierocratic societies that make no attempt to shape that society as a whole (perhaps because they have no opportunity to do so). A paradigmatic instance of such an institutional religion is that of Judaism, during the periods in which it existed as a minority community within Christian or Muslim societies.

My third variety of religion is what I shall call "modern" religion. This is the form of religion characteristic of the secular states established by the European and North American political revolutions of the eighteenth century. In early forms of modern religion, religious affiliation – one's confessional allegiance – was an important source of identity. But modern religion has increasingly become a matter of personal choice. While distinct communities continue to exist, movement from one to another has become relatively easy. Modern religious practice may involve participation in the life of an institutional religion, although many such religions have renounced their hierocratic aims. But it can also involve what I shall call "post-institutional" religion: participation in loosely organized and informal religious groups, such as the Wiccan and neo-pagan movements of modern Western societies.

1.4 A Multifaceted Relation

Given the very different forms taken by both *scientia* and religion, it should already be clear that one cannot make general claims about their relation. ("What is the relation between *scientia* and religion?" "Well, it depends.") There is a further difficulty about generalizations, which has to do with the different facets, the different dimensions of the relationship. I shall discuss four such dimensions.

The first is what I shall call the *cognitive* dimension, which has to do with the content of scientific theories and religious doctrines. It is in this context that the question of conflict often arises. Seventeenth-century Christians asked whether Christian beliefs were compatible with the Copernican theory; modern Christians have asked if they are compatible with a belief in evolution. In discussing the cognitive dimension of the relationship, we should remember that religions themselves are not monolithic. The central beliefs of historic religions are embodied in sacred texts, which are differently interpreted by different believers. Similar issues arise regarding our understanding of *scientia*. Before we can decide whether religious and scientific ideas are in conflict, we need to decide what a particular *scientia* is telling us. Can it, for instance, tell us about realities that are inaccessible to observation? Or are its claims limited to what can be observed? Is the authority of *scientia* limited to particular domains? Or can its methods be applied to any question we may wish to ask?

A second dimension of the *scientia* and religion relation I shall refer to as *teleological*, from the Greek *telos*, meaning an "end" or a "goal." *Pace* Stephen Jay Gould (2001), religious and scientific communities have overlapping but not identical goals. Both aim at knowledge: they seek to make justified assertions about the way the world is. Some traditional forms of *scientia* (such as integral cosmologies) and most religions also have ethical goals. They go beyond telling us how the world is, to tell us how we ought to behave. Some religions also seek to bring about the salvation of individuals, liberating them from their present state of suffering. Christian theologians refer to the doctrine of salvation as "soteriology." If we adopt this term, we can say that most religions and some forms of *scientia* have *ethical* and *soteriological* as well as *cognitive* goals. It may seem surprising to suggest that a *scientia* can have ethical and soteriological goals, since modern science has largely abandoned these. But as we shall see, a narrow focus on cognitive goals is one of its distinctive characteristics.

The *scientia* and religion relation also has what I shall call an *organizational* dimension. Religion is a communal affair. However much religious beliefs are internalized, they are internalized only after being inherited. Like my mother tongue, my initial religious beliefs were inherited from my family and the community to which they belonged. But a *scientia*, too, is a communal affair. This is particularly clear in the case of modern science, since its development is inseparable from the growth of scientific societies. So any discussion of *scientia* and religion must take into account the kinds of organization in which they are embodied. The memberships of scientific and religious organizations may overlap, insofar as there are scientists who are also religious. But scientific organizations have a very different character from religious ones. Members of each will engage in distinctive kinds of activity, which are shaped by differing norms: different expectations regarding behavior.

Finally, the *scientia* and religion relation has an *epistemological* dimension, "epistemology" being the theory of knowledge. There are three issues I shall discuss under this heading. A first has to do with the kind of knowledge that a *scientia* or a religion may claim to offer. Is it procedural or declarative knowledge: "knowing how" to perform a certain action or "knowing that" some state of affairs obtains? If it is both, how do these relate to one another? A second issue has to do with the idiom in which scientific and religious claims are expressed. While scientists may employ narrative and metaphor when developing their theories (and when speaking to nonscientists), they prefer literal forms of speech: arguments rather than storytelling. Religions, by way of contrast, have always preferred narrative to argument, embrace apparent paradoxes, and rely heavily on the kinds of language that scientists try to avoid. A third epistemological issue has to do with our *sources* of knowledge. Many religions demand a commitment from their devotees: an act of faith by which one "takes refuge" (as Buddhists say) in the teachings of their founder. What is the relation between what is known by faith and what can be known by reason? Does a reliance on faith make religion different from *scientia*?

1.5 Conditional Conclusions

I said earlier that it would be foolish to try to make general claims about "science" and "religion." More precisely, while we can make some general claims, these will need to be of a conditional kind. They will state that if the religion is question is of kind *x*, and the *scientia* in question is of kind *y*, then they will be related in manner *z*. Conclusions of this kind are unlikely to make headlines or produce a bestseller. But they may still be true. It may be possible to make further suggestions. I shall suggest, for instance, that the most significant differences between *scientia* and religion lie on the level of epistemology. When conflicts occur between scientific and religious communities, it can most commonly be traced back to their differing conceptions of how we attain knowledge.

If you have read this far, you will have some idea of the direction in which we are heading. The discussion that follows will be structured according to the four dimensions of the *scientia* and religion relation: the cognitive, organizational, teleological, and epistemological. Under each heading, I shall argue that the relation between *scientia* and religion is a function of the differing kinds of *scientia* and the differing kinds of religion in question.

This Element claims to be nothing more than a provisional sketch, a first attempt at "deprovincializing" the science and religion literature. There may be better ways of organizing this material; there is certainly more material that could be included. But I make this attempt because I am convinced of its importance. Most of us are aware that our locally dominant form of religion – the Christianity that most readers will be familiar with – is only one among many. But we may not be aware that our form of *scientia* is also just one among many. As my final remarks will suggest, a realization of this fact may contribute to a resolution of the ecological crisis of our age, which may be the most important crisis humanity has faced.

2 The Cognitive Dimension

The first dimension of the *scientia* and religion relation is the cognitive one. It has to do with the propositions defended by a particular *scientia* and the beliefs underlying the practices of a particular religion. If you have read my introductory remarks, you will not be surprised to hear that the relation between these two will differ, according to the kind of religion and the kind of *scientia* in question.

2.1 Small-Scale Societies

There are societies that have no *scientia*, in the sense I have defined. They have no tradition of inquiry that aims to create a systematic account of the principles governing the natural or human world. These are the communities commonly known today as "small-scale" societies, which exist by hunting and gathering or subsistence agriculture. It is tempting to think that life in such societies would be like the "state of nature" imagined by the seventeenth-century philosopher Thomas Hobbes: "solitary, poor, nasty, brutish, and short" (Hobbes 1998: 84 [1.8.9]). But this would be too hasty a conclusion. Anthropologists who have studied hunter-gatherer societies argue that their way of life is a successful adaptation to the environment in which they live (Lee 1968: 43). One has even described their way of life as that of "the original affluent society" (Sahlins 1974).

Unsurprisingly, this idea has been contested (Kaplan 2000). But even its most vigorous critics have not returned to a Hobbesian view. They recognize that life in such societies was generally tolerable and at least sometimes pleasant. Societies that follow this way of life have also survived for very long periods of time (Suzman 2017: 41), much longer, in fact, than our modern industrial society, whose future is by no means assured. So they must have been doing some things well.

2.1.1 Traditional Knowledge

One reason for the long-term survival of small-scale societies is religious. Even if they had no system of central government of the kind Hobbes thought essential, they had equivalent hierarchies of metapersons, who formed what we may call "the original political society." As one scholar puts it, "there are kingly beings in heaven even where there are no chiefs on earth" (Sahlins 2017: 91). But a second reason for their success was that such societies had extensive bodies of knowledge about their environment. We find such knowledge even today among people who live by hunting and gathering or subsistence agriculture. Among the Achuar people of the Amazon region, for instance, a young man of relatively little hunting experience "is able to identify by sight several hundred kinds of birds, to imitate their song, and to describe their habits and habitat" and can "recognize a trail from the slightest of signs, such as a butterfly hovering at the foot of a tree, attracted by the still fresh urine of a monkey that has recently passed" (Descola 2013: 100).

Knowledge of this kind comes close, at times, to meeting my definition of a *scientia*. Take, for instance, the traditional navigational knowledge of Polynesian peoples. This was a complex body of knowledge that was taught in a systematic fashion to aspiring practitioners. Navigators needed to know, for instance, which stars or constellations appeared at particular points on the horizon, forming "star-paths" across the sky. Does this count as a form of *scientia*? Perhaps it does, although it differs from a *scientia* insofar as it did not create a tradition of research and was often kept secret, being the exclusive possession of certain families or groups (Lewis 1994: 8). So even if navigational knowledge borders on being a form of *scientia*, I shall regard it as a form of traditional knowledge.

As I noted earlier, the term "traditional knowledge" embraces four categories of belief and practice. It embraces (a) classificatory schemes relating to plants and animals, (b) stories about the origins of natural objects, (c) beliefs regarding the properties of natural objects, and (d) practical know-how. (Combinations of these are also possible, navigational knowledge being an example.) The first of these categories is perhaps the most familiar to students of anthropology, for it forms much of what is discussed under the heading of "ethnoscience." Some scholars have suggested that such classificatory schemes follow a common pattern across cultures (Berlin 1992: 8–9). But more recent studies favor the idea that there are a plurality of such schemes, shaped by local beliefs and interests (Lloyd 2007: 48–57; Ludwig 2018a: 417–19).

Even if the classificatory schemes employed in small-scale societies were universal, the same could not be said of stories of origin. While some etiological tales are widely diffused, they take on differing forms in different societies. We may be inclined to regard such stories as religious. While they begin by describing the observable features of living things and their environment, they commonly trace these back to a mythic past and to stories about superhuman beings. The Australian Aboriginal stories of the "Dreaming" are perhaps the best known example. But there are many others. The Māori people of New Zealand, for instance, have genealogies (*whakapapa*), not just of human beings, but also of plants and animals, genealogies that go back to the mythic time of creation (Haami & Roberts 2002). This means that when we are dealing with such stories, we cannot make a sharp distinction between religious and secular beliefs. Such knowledge relates to *both* the realm of the gods *and* the natural world.

Alongside classificatory knowledge and stories of origin, traditional knowledge includes knowledge regarding the properties of natural objects. Some of this will also resemble what we think of as scientific knowledge. Most small-scale societies, for instance, have beliefs regarding the healing properties of particular plants. Insofar as these properties can be discovered by trial and error, such beliefs are likely to be similar across cultures. But other beliefs about the properties of natural objects are unable to be tested in this way. These include, for instance, beliefs about what distinguishes living from nonliving beings (the *mauri* of Māori tradition) or the idea that some nonhuman beings have an interior life similar to ours ("animism," as it is commonly known). While beliefs of this kind are found across cultures, they are by no means universal. Insofar as they deal with hidden powers, accessed by ritual, these beliefs could also be thought of as "religious."

Finally, traditional knowledge involves practical know-how – knowledge of how to fish, garden, navigate, or build a canoe – which is passed on, either freely or to bodies of experts, from one generation to the next. Such knowledge is transmitted for the most part by imitation, by means of a more or less formal apprenticeship. While the know-how in question may be partly spelled out in words, its mastery is largely a matter of practice rather than explicit teaching. Some of this savoir-faire will also fall into our category of the religious, since success may be thought to depend on proper behavior towards spiritual powers. Navigational knowledge, for instance, may include the practice of regarding certain activities as *tapu* ("taboo") or information about spirits who can guide the navigator (Genz 2017: 213). Such knowledge is likely to be culturally specific. But insofar as it deals with this-worldly matters, we might expect a kind of "convergent evolution," as differing societies may arrive independently at similar technical solutions to common problems.

2.1.2 Religious Beliefs

What about the religious beliefs of small-scale societies? Their religious beliefs are generally what I shall call "embedded beliefs," closely tied to particular practices that have tangible goals. By "embedded beliefs," I mean that they are largely implicit in the practices in question, particularly ritual practices. The beliefs underlying the practices are sometimes made explicit. But they are made explicit only insofar as this is required for ritual practice and to ensure that they can be passed on to the next generation of ritual practitioners: the priests or shamans of the tribe.

To some extent, this is true of all popular religion: what we might call religion "on the ground." It, too, consists of beliefs embodied in practices. Even when these beliefs are spelled out and made explicit, most practitioners feel no need to shape them into a single, coherent system. The systematization of religious beliefs is attempted (if at all) only by small groups of philosophers and theologians, with whom the ordinary practitioner may have little contact. But while this is true of all religion, it is particular clear in the case of small-scale societies, whose members rarely (if ever) create a systematic theology out of their religious practices.

Not only are such beliefs not brought into a systematic relation with one another, but their application tends to be context-dependent. They are not brought to bear on all the situations to which (it seems) they could be applied. Again, this is particularly evident in small-scale societies, which have no systematic theology. But it is not unique to such societies. A modern theist, for instance, may claim to believe that God is omnipresent, but there are contexts in which God's presence is never invoked (Pyssiäinen 2003: 118). Belief in God's omnipresence will be triggered only in particular circumstances, such as when believers are assessing their own behavior or feel a need to invoke his assistance.

This may seem odd, for we are inclined to think of our beliefs as simple facts. We either believe something or we do not. But beliefs are better thought of as dispositions to act or respond in certain ways. Some such dispositions are active in (practically) all relevant circumstances. Every time I walk across the floor, I act on the assumption it will continue to support my weight. Every time I walk into my local store, I assume I will be able to make a purchase. But other dispositions do not always shape my behavior, even in circumstances that would allow them to do so. I may, for instance, be disposed to think negatively of black people. In most circumstances, I may treat black and white people alike. Yet when faced with an approaching figure in a dark alley, I may become more fearful if that person is black. Religious beliefs tend to be of this kind. They are dispositions to respond in certain ways whose activation is context-dependent.

We find a striking example of such context-dependency among the Vezo community, a semi-nomadic people living on the southern coast of Madagascar. Members of this community have two conceptions of death. One of these suggests that when a person dies all bodily and psychological functions cease; the other holds that at least psychological functions continue. But these tend to be activated in different contexts, the religious conception being linked with ritual practices (Astuti & Harris 2008: 733). Once again, this is not restricted to small-scale societies, for a similar phenomenon was observed among modern Spanish schoolchildren (Harris & Giménez 2005: 153–4).

2.1.3 Traditional Knowledge and Religion

These remarks about belief may feel like a digression. But they help us to understand the relation between traditional knowledge ("ethnoscience," if you like) and religion. There are three factors to take into account when discussing this relation. The first has to do with the categories of knowledge employed. The second has to do with the context-dependent character of religious belief. The third has to do with the content of traditional knowledge schemes.

Let me begin with the categories employed. In any society, there may be instances of what psychologists call "cognitive dissonance": tensions between differing propositions that are both held to be true. But one will not think of such tensions as relating to *science* and *religion* (or even *scientia* and religion) unless one has these categories to hand. Members of small-scale lacked these categories, or at least did so before they were introduced by outsiders. They have categories of their own, but these cut across the science and religion divide. Māori people, for instance, traditionally spoke of two domains of knowledge, represented by the upper jawbone (*te kauwae runga*) and the lower jawbone (*te kauwae raro*). The first referred to celestial matters, the second to the world of humans. While this resembles our distinction between religion and science, it is by no means identical with it, for the knowledge related to the "lower jawbone" included information about spiritual beings (*atua*) concerned with earthly affairs (Best 1976: 200). Similarly, the people of the Lamotrek atoll in Micronesia distinguish between what we may call "secular" and "sacred" knowledge (*reeipy* and *rong*). But navigational knowledge, which in some respects resembles a *scientia*, is "sacred" knowledge because of its origin in the spirit world (Metzgar 2008: 105).

A second factor is the context-dependent character of many beliefs. Even if there is an incompatibility between differing sets of beliefs, this may not be noticed if they are activated in differing contexts. The Jigalong people, a Western Desert Australian aboriginal group, have two distinct explanations of parenthood: one physiological (involving sexual relations) and the other religious (involving spirit children who enter the womb via the mother's thumb or toenail or mouth). But the two are "invoked independently, never interdependently or as competing explanations of the same phenomenon" (Tonkinson 1978: 85). The Dorze people of Ethiopia claim that leopards are Christians who observe the fasts of the Ethiopian Orthodox Church. But this representation is not activated when it comes to guarding one's animals, for the Dorze are "no less careful to guard [their] animals on Wednesdays and Fridays, [which are] fast days, than on the other days of the week" (Sperber 1975: 94).

The third factor has to do with the character of the beliefs and practices we would call "scientific" and "religious." While these can overlap and compete, often they do not. This is particularly the case when it comes to practical know-how. The Trobriand Islanders, living to the east of Papua New Guinea, employed both practical knowledge and magic in making their *waga* (canoes). But they understood that in building a canoe "magic, however efficient, will not make up for bad workmanship" (Malinowski 2014: 125). Both means were employed. A similar complementarity can be found in matters of belief. Take, for instance, etiological tales. While these stories commonly trace features of the observable world to the world of the gods, they are not in competition with either classificatory knowledge or practical know-how. They take classificatory knowledge as their starting point without contesting it. The same is true of totemic classifications, which "ride piggy-back" on folk-biological categories (Atran 1998: 557). In such contexts, religious beliefs and traditional knowledge of the natural world can coexist, being applied in a complementary fashion in pursuit of similar goals.

2.2 An Integral Cosmology

So much for small-scale societies. A different kind of relation between scientific and religious beliefs is characteristic of societies that have an integral cosmology. What distinguishes such a cosmology from the traditional knowledge of small-scale societies is that its principles are spelled out in a systematic fashion, by thinkers whom we call "philosophers" or (better still) "sages." The clearest instance of such a society is that of China. As I noted earlier, from the fifth century BCE until to first century CE, a number of Chinese thinkers developed a striking example of an integral cosmology. This was an "integral" cosmology insofar as it included human actions within its view of the world, offering principles of correct action as well as descriptions of how the world operates.

2.2.1 A Correlative Cosmology

I have already distinguished this cosmology from science, as we know it, while assuming that it remains a form of *scientia*. Some may hesitate to go even this far, preferring to call it a "speculative metaphysics" (Fung 2009: 277). But the use of this phrase seems inappropriate. Our distinction between physics and metaphysics goes back to Aristotle, who regarded metaphysics as the study of entities and principles that do not undergo alteration and physics as the study of the changing world and its causes (Aristotle 1925: 296 [1026a14–18]). Such a distinction is foreign to classical Chinese thought (Perkins 2016: sect. 1). The principles developed by ancient Chinese cosmologists did not distinguish between that which changes and that which is unchanging. They were expressions of the way the natural world can be seen to unfold (Schwartz 1985: 360).

What were the principles of this integral cosmology? The best known are the contrasting but mutually dependent categories known as *yīn* and *yáng* and the idea of a fundamental substance known as *qì* (or *ch'i*) underlying all things. But they also included the varying relations of *gǎnyìng* ("resonance") that existed between classes of objects, and an understanding of change by way of the *wǔxíng* (*wu-hsing*).[1] The last of these terms refers to the five "elemental phases" of wood, fire, earth, metal, and water (Pankenier 2013: 7). Another principle, particularly important in medicine, was the idea of the human body as a microcosm, mirroring the order of the cosmos as a whole (Wang 2012: 175).

This cosmology had considerable explanatory power, even if its explanations seem fanciful by the standards of modern science. The five elemental phases provided an explanation of historical change, as each of the elements was seen to dominate a particular period. Other phenomena could be understood in terms of the increase and decrease of varieties of *qì*. Still other explanations relied on correlative thinking, in which the properties and powers of objects are thought to depend on relations of similarity and contrast (Graham 1989: 320). To take a simple example, in the *Huáinánzi*, compiled under the leadership of Liú Ān (179–122 BCE), birds are opposed to fish as fire is opposed to water. This is taken to explain why a startled bird moves (like fire) upwards, while a startled fish moves (like water) downward (Graham 1989: 334).

As in the case of small-scale societies, a cosmology of this kind cuts across our distinctions between "science" and "religion." First, its functions overlapped those of religion. It sought not merely to describe, predict, and control the course of events, but also to shape human behavior. Second, it had religious roots. Its origins lay in the writings of specialists in what were known as *shùshù fāngjì*, "calculations and recipes" (Doar 2010: 14). These were people with technical skills in a variety of fields: divination, rituals, astronomy and astrology, calendar-making, music, and medicine (Wang 2000: 78–9, 123). One of its

---

[1] I have employed the pinyin system of transliteration for Chinese terms, but when a word is first used I have included the Wade-Giles version in brackets.

foundational texts, the *Yìjīng* (*I-Ching*), was originally a divination manual. Third, while broadly naturalistic, this cosmology was often combined with explicitly religious ideas. In this sense, it is not wholly "secular." It will be worth pausing for a moment to examine some examples of what looks to us like a "mixing of genres."

2.2.2 Cosmology and the Gods

The tendency of Chinese correlative cosmology was towards a nonreligious view of the world. Although not "naturalistic" in a modern sense, it did explain phenomena by reference to intrinsic principles (such as *yīn* and *yáng*, *qì*, and the *wǔxíng*) rather than the actions of the gods. We see this in the development of medical thought. During the Shang dynasty (ca. 1765–1123 BCE) and into the Warring States, Qin, and Han periods, illness was commonly regarded as evidence of the ill-will of ancestors or of possession by demons. But in the canonical medical text, the *Huángdì Nèijīng* (*Huang-ti ne-ching*; Inner Canon of the Yellow Emperor), compiled in the first century BCE, explanations of disease appeal to aspects of the natural world (Harper 1990: 210–11).

Despite this naturalistic tendency, ideas and practices we would think of as religious continue to exist alongside those we would regard as (broadly) scientific (Harper 1999: 875). In many texts, for instance, ideas about "ghosts and spirits" (*guǐshén*) were found alongside descriptions of natural principles (Harper 1999: 831). This persistence of religious ideas within an apparently naturalistic cosmology can be illustrated by reference to an idea central to many schools of Chinese philosophy, that of *tiān* (heaven).

The term *tiān* is used in classical texts in a variety of ways. In some contexts, it was used to refer simply to the "heavens" or "sky": the upper part of the cosmos. But it was also used to refer to the power thought to lie behind the "great pattern" (*dàlǐ*): the proper order of human conduct. Understood in this way, *tiān* was seen as the source of authority in human society, which was conveyed through the *tiānmìng*, the "mandate of heaven." When represented in this way, *tiān* took over some of the functions, and even some of the characteristics, of the supreme deity *Dì* (Lord) or *Shàngdì* (Lord-on-High), who had been worshipped in China during the Shang period (Ching 1993: 33–4). In these contexts, it seems appropriate to capitalize the initial letter of the corresponding English word, reflecting the quasi-divine character of the reality in question.

I say "quasi-divine" because Heaven was never thought of as entirely "transcendent," in the sense of separate from the observable world (Perkins 2016: sect. 2). But Heaven was sometimes thought of a personal being, responding purposefully to human behavior. We find this religious concept of Heaven in the work of the philosopher Mòzǐ (470–391 BC), who writes that *tiān* "desires righteousness and abhors unrighteousness," watches over human affairs, and rewards correct behavior (Johnston 2010: 233–4 [26.2]). By way of contrast, the Confucian writer Xúnzǐ (313–238 BC) uses *tiān* in ways that are less clearly religious. In his writings, *tiān* refers to the nonpurposeful order of change in the nonhuman world. While this "natural" order continues to have normative significance, particularly when it comes to ritual action, the old idea of a purposeful deity has faded into the background (Eno 1990: 154–69).

This ambivalence about the character of heaven can be found even in some of the leading proponents of classical cosmology. Of particular interest here is the work of Dǒng Zhòngshū (Tung Chung-shu) (179–104 BCE), who combined Confucian ideals with correlative thinking (Schwartz 1985: 363). On some occasions, Dǒng describes the responses of heaven in ways that seem mechanical and impersonal (Fung 1953: 57–8). But in others, he depicts Heaven as a personal deity, writing (for instance) that "Heaven has its own feelings of joy and anger, and a mind [which experiences] sadness or pleasure, analogous to those of man" (Fung 1953: 30). So even Dǒng's cosmology never entirely loses its religious dimension.

2.3 Natural Philosophy

I have argued that the cosmology developed in China during the Warring States period and the Qin and former Han dynasties is an integral cosmology. It has a normative (action-guiding) as well as an explanatory role and it never entirely loses its religious aspects. What I want to discuss now is a different kind of *scientia*. It is one whose claims about the natural world *are* distinguished from talk about divinity and from discussions of appropriate behavior, but which forms part of a larger intellectual project in which these all find a home. I shall refer to a science of this kind as "natural philosophy." It has its roots in the ancient Greek world, but finds its fullest expression in the universities of late medieval Europe.

2.3.1 The Branches of Learning

I have already noted Aristotle's distinction between science and metaphysics, metaphysics being the study of entities that do not undergo alteration, while physics is the study of the changing world and its causes. But this was not the only distinction Aristotle made between the various branches of learning.

Aristotle and his followers understood "science" (in Greek *epistēmē*, in Latin *scientia*) in a broad sense, to refer to any body of demonstrated knowledge. But these bodies of knowledge differed in kind. The broadest division was that between *theoretical* sciences (including natural philosophy), which sought knowledge for its own sake, *practical* sciences (such as ethics), which had to do with proper conduct, and the *productive* sciences, which aimed to produce beautiful or useful objects (Aristotle 1925: 295 [1025b25]). It is within the domain of the theoretical sciences that we find metaphysics and physics, as well as mathematics. Aristotle's natural philosophy was a theoretical science, which included the study of both general principles (found in works such as the *Physics*) and more specialized phenomena. His more specialized studies included works on phenomena in the upper atmosphere ("meteorology") and extensive writings on what we would call "biology."

Aristotle's distinctions were adopted by the late medieval authors who taught in the newly founded universities. Thomas Aquinas (1225–74), for instance, endorsed the distinctions made by both Aristotle and the early medieval writer Boethius (480–524 CE) between three types of theoretical science. The first of Aquinas's categories is physics, which he also calls "natural science" (*scientia naturalis*), the second mathematics, and the third metaphysics, which Aquinas also calls "theology or divine science" (Aquinas 1986: 14 [5.1]). Not only does Aquinas distinguish these; he even suggests that these different sciences should be learned at different stages in life. A young person, he writes, can scarcely understand natural philosophy, let alone ethics and theology (Aquinas 1986: 100–1 [lect. 1]).

The details of this classificatory system need not detain us, but there are two points I want to make about it. The first has to do with the unity of knowledge. One of the features of Aristotle's philosophy was that it employed a common set of explanatory principles across the whole range of the sciences. These included the distinctions between form and matter and actuality and potentiality, as well as the doctrine of final causes (the goals towards which processes tend). Such principles could be applied, albeit in differing ways, in fields as diverse as metaphysics, astronomy, politics, physics, and ethics (Lloyd 1968: 293–4). This made the study of the natural world part of a larger enterprise (Hinchman & Hinchman 1991: 465), which culminated in the knowledge of "things divine" or "theology." The theology in question was not the study of the "sacred page," that is to say, a theology derived from an assumed divine revelation. (Aristotle had no belief in a divine revelation.) It is what we would call a *philosophical* theology, which deals with what can be known about divinity by "mere" human reason.

My second point is that despite this sense of the unity of knowledge, the distinctions remained important. The differing forms of knowledge were not confused. While Aristotle employed some common explanatory principles, he also recognized that these needed to be applied in differing ways in different fields (Lennox 2001: 134). One cannot study astronomy or optics, for instance, in the same way as one would study living organisms. Similar remarks may be made about the distinction between physics and metaphysics. The two were certainly continuous, but were different kinds of study, undertaken at different times and in different works. Although Aristotle's *Physics* establishes the need for an unmoved mover, he identifies this being with God only in his *Metaphysics* (Lang 1989: 576). In the medieval universities, these distinctions were reinforced by the fact that much teaching in the faculties of arts was by way of commentaries on the books of Aristotle. Insofar as Aristotle avoids talk of God in his *libri naturales* – his works on natural philosophy – so did his medieval followers when commenting on those works.

This is not to say there were no crossovers between disciplines. Such crossovers were possible precisely because of a belief in the unity of knowledge. A striking feature of fourteenth-century physics, for instance, is its focus on measurement. Writers of this period applied conceptions of measurement not only to physical realities – motion, heat, light, and color – but also to "less tractable qualities such as love, charity, [and] beauty" (Murdoch 1974: 64). But this belief in the unity of knowledge coexisted with the conviction that each field of knowledge had its own rules. Nicole Oresme (1320–82), for instance, complained about the way in which "some theologians" were misusing notions of measurement drawn from physics. They were speaking about the "latitude" of charity, using a term drawn from physics, when charity (he argued) is not the kind of reality to which this term can be applied (Oresme 1968: 171 [I.3]).

Why is this important? I have argued that all peoples have two ways of regarding the natural world: one drawn from observation and the other from traditions regarding "metapersons": gods, spirits, and ancestors. But many societies do not clearly distinguish these. What we see in Aristotelian thinking is the beginning of a distinction between what we call "scientific" and "religious" knowledge. The distinction is nicely illustrated by writings on optics, which was an important field within late medieval natural philosophy. The study of light was sometimes thought to have religious implications. Robert Grosseteste (1165–1253), for instance, believed that the light (*lumen*) studied within optics was dependent for its existence on the simple substance also called "light" (*lux*), which (according to Genesis) God created before the sun and stars (Riedl 1942: 5). But when the same Grosseteste came to discuss the cause of a phenomenon such as the rainbow, his explanation made no reference to God (Eastwood 1968: 317–20). It referred only to physical factors, namely the refraction of light as it passes from one medium to another.

2.3.2 Two Types of Theology

We have seen that although natural philosophy was not confused with theology or metaphysics, it did form part of a larger project. That larger philosophical project included metaphysics: the discussion of "first principles" and "first causes," which were regarded as divine. Insofar as these principles and causes were regarded as divine, metaphysics was a *theological* enterprise, in a broad sense of this term. One might think that this would lead towards a harmony of scientific and religious claims, a view of the world that integrated talk of the natural and the divine. It would not be an *integral* cosmology such as that found in ancient China, which did not make these distinctions. But it would be an *integrated* one, which drew together the results of what were regarded as differing forms of inquiry.

What complicates this story is that there were two uses of the term "theology." The first use, in which "theology" is used to refer to metaphysics, is a pre-Christian one, which is found in Aristotle (1925: 296 [1026a19–20]). As we might expect, this theology *was* integrated with other forms of knowledge. But there developed, in both Christian and Muslim contexts, a different kind of theology. This was not based on philosophical reflection. It was based on the study of those matters that were thought to be divinely revealed. In the Christian case, this type of theology was founded on sacred scripture and the teachings of the church. In the Muslim case, a theology of this kind (known as *kalām*), was founded on the Qur'an, regarded as divine speech, and the *ahādīth*, the reports of the actions and words of Muhammad.

Since these two kinds of theology relied on differing sources of knowledge – philosophical reason, on the one hand, and religious faith, on the other – they were taught (in Europe) within different university faculties. Neither was there any guarantee they would be compatible. Indeed, sometimes they were not. The biblical and Qur'anic doctrine of creation, for instance, came into conflict with Aristotle's belief that the world had no beginning (Grant 1974: 48 [art. 87]). The Christian doctrine of the immortality of the soul was not obviously compatible with Aristotelian physics (Lohr 1991: 51–2). Even Aristotle's "unmoved mover" was not simply identical with the Christian God. Some theological sleight of hand was needed in order to identify them (Dawes 2016: 32–3).

There is a certain irony in this situation. Modern scientists for the most part attempt to set aside metaphysical questions. They try to avoid engaging in debates about what "really exists." This reduces the likelihood that scientific claims will come into conflict with religious ones. Modern science simply does not speak about God, even as "primary cause" or "first mover." Aristotelian philosophy, by way of contrast, did speak about God. For precisely this reason, it had more chance than does modern science of coming into conflict with a theology based on an assumed divine revelation.

Medieval religious thinkers were well aware of this danger. In both the Christian and Muslim worlds, it led them to restrict the kind of philosophy that could be undertaken. In 1272, for instance, the Faculty of Arts at the University of Paris forbade its scholars from discussing "any purely theological question" (Grant 1974: 44–5). It also commanded that if scholars did discuss theological questions that fell within the scope of philosophy, they were to resolve such discussions in favor of the faith. The medieval Muslim theologian Abū Hāmid Muhammad al-Ghazālī (1058–1111) was similarly concerned to downplay the competence of philosophy in matters religious, so as to leave room for divine revelation (Griffel 2009: 98–100).

2.4 Science and Religion

We have seen that *scientia* as natural philosophy formed part of a larger body of knowledge. While having a certain autonomy, it was thought of as contributing to our knowledge of things divine. But we have also seen that this picture is complicated by the emergence of a different kind of theology. This was referred to by Christians as the study of the "sacred page" and by Muslims as *ilm al-kalām*, the study of the speech of God. In this context, the terms "science" and "religion" can be understood as referring to distinct bodies of knowledge, drawing on differing kinds of evidence and developing according to differing principles.

2.4.1 Overlapping Domains

What is the relation between science and religion, so conceived? Stephen Jay Gould was mistaken in holding that scientific and religious claims belong to differing domains, which never overlap. There are, of course, some scientific claims that will have no bearing on matters of faith, just as there are religious claims that have no bearing on science. I know of no religion that is anything but indifferent to Boyle's Law, which states the relation between the pressure of a gas and the volume of the container in which it is found. Even when it comes to the study of the heavens, religions may be indifferent to scientific findings regarding which their scriptures are silent. Al-Ghazālī, for instance, remarked that the (Ptolemaic) theory of the lunar eclipse "does not clash with any religious doctrine" and is therefore unproblematic from the point of view of the believer (al-Ghazālī 2000: 5–6).

It is when the claims of science and those of faith do overlap that apparent conflicts can be found. Practically all modern biologists, for example, accept that the diversity of species is the result of an evolutionary process whose primary mechanism is natural selection. At least some religious believers, by way of contrast, hold that individual species were directly created by God. Even those who accept the biological theory of evolution tend to do so only with modifications. Pope John Paul II, for instance, made it clear that evolution applies only to the development of the human body, the soul being immediately created by God (John Paul II 1997: 383). This is not a scientifically irrelevant claim, as Michael Ruse argues (Ruse 1997: 334), for in Roman Catholic thought the soul is responsible for our powers of thought and moral judgment. It follows that when evolutionary theory is used to offer natural explanations of our cognitive powers, such explanations are in conflict with Roman Catholic teaching.

These are clear cases of at least apparent conflict between science and religion. I say "apparent conflict" because theistic thinkers cannot concede that the conflict here is a real one. The "book of nature," as medieval Christians used to say, is written by God, the creator of the natural world, and therefore cannot contradict the book of revelation of which God is also the author. So the theological question then becomes how one deals with such apparent conflicts.

2.4.2 Dealing with Apparent Conflict

There are several options here. First, religious thinkers can try to cast doubt on the science. They can do so directly, by arguing that the scientific conclusions are not supported by the evidence. A popular move here is to try to cast doubt on the methods, tools, or techniques that scientists employ. The opponents of Galileo, for instance, noted that what he appeared to observe through his telescope could be an artifact of the instrument itself (Drake 1980: 44–5). Today's young-earth creationists seek to impugn the reliability of carbon-dating techniques or the uniformitarian assumptions of modern geology (Whitcomb & Morris 1961: 43–4, 223–4). As we have seen, some Christian philosophers go so far as to argue that modern science as a whole is tainted by atheistic assumptions.

Believers can also cast doubt on the science indirectly, by arguing for certain limitations on scientific knowledge. Young-earth creationists, for instance, sometimes argue that scientific claims should be limited to matters that can be reproduced experimentally (Whitcomb & Morris 1961: 219). Because we cannot reproduce major evolutionary changes experimentally, a theory that proposes such changes cannot be truly scientific. A more sophisticated version of this approach involves adopting an "instrumentalist" view of science. This holds that scientific theories are no more than instruments that allow us to predict what is able to be observed. They do not tell us what the world is really like (Duhem 1962: 21). It is this approach that Cardinal Bellarmine, the head of the Roman Inquisition, unsuccessfully urged on Galileo (Dawes 2016: 67–8).

The alternative to casting doubt on the science is to reinterpret the religious doctrines with which the science appears to be in conflict. But when is the believer permitted to do this? A tradition of Christian thought dating back to St. Augustine (354–430 CE), employs two principles in making this decision. The first is what we may call "the principle of the priority of demonstration" (McMullin 1998: 294). This holds that where a scientific claim incompatible with the literal sense of sacred scripture is demonstrated that is to say, established beyond doubt), the scriptural passage must be reinterpreted. St. Augustine, for instance, is prepared to understand the word "light" in Gen 1:3 in a nonliteral sense, to avoid contradicting what is "certain from reason and experience" (Augustine 1982: 38, 42 [1,17.32, 1.19.39]).

A problem arises, however, when the scientific claim is not established beyond doubt. At this point, the same tradition of interpretation invokes what we may call "the principle of the priority of Scripture" (McMullin 1998: 295). This holds that when a scientific claim incompatible with the literal sense of scripture has not been demonstrated, the literal sense of scripture is to be maintained. It is this second principle that contributed to the Catholic Church's condemnation of the Copernican theory in 1616, for at that time Copernicus's view lacked demonstrative proof. The difficulty here is knowing what "demonstrated beyond doubt" means, a problem that may have contributed to Galileo's conflict with the Church (Dawes 2016: 95–7).

3 The Goals of Science and Religion

So much for the cognitive dimension of the science and religion relation. What we have found is that not all societies have a clear distinction between "scientific" and "religious" beliefs. The distinction is lacking in small-scale societies and was blurred within the integral cosmology of ancient China. It does develop in the history of European thought, with both Aristotle's distinctions between differing kinds of knowledge and the development of a theology based on an assumed divine revelation. This set the scene for apparent conflicts between the two, although medieval thinkers also developed principles for adjudicating such disputes.

It is time to turn to the second dimension of the science and religion relation, which I am describing as *teleological*. What are the goals pursued by different forms of both *scientia* and religion? How do these goals relate to one another?

3.1 A Variety of Goals

Philosophers have commonly focused on what we may call the *epistemic goals* of science and religion, that is to say, the ways in which both aim at achieving knowledge. I have already discussed the cognitive dimension of the science and religion relation. I shall later discuss the differing ways in which scientific and religious claims are expressed and the sources from which their knowledge claims are drawn. So I shall say no more about epistemic goals here.

When it comes to *non-epistemic goals* of both science and religion, we may distinguish between (a) *well-being* goals and (b) *normative* aims. Well-being goals have to do with benefits promised to the individual or community as a result of a particular practice. The promised benefits may be categorized in three ways. They may be (i) this-worldly (such as a good harvest) or other-worldly (such as release from the cycle of rebirth). They may be (ii) individual (such as recovery from illness) or communal (such as collective victory over an enemy. They may (iii) involve the maintenance of an existing state of affairs (such as protection from death) or the introduction of a radically new state of affairs (as in the coming of God's kingdom). Such goals can also be combined. Some this-worldly benefits, for instance, such as such as success in hunting, may be related to the activities of individuals or small groups. But other equally this-worldly benefits, such as victory over one's enemies, may be promised to the community as a whole.

The second major category of non-epistemic goals consists of those that are *normative*, which have to do with how things ought to be. These normative goals may be associated with the well-being goals just discussed, for the benefits promised by a practice may be dependent on the correct behavior of the individual or community. (A good harvest, for example, may be thought to be dependent on making the correct sacrifices. Eternal life may be regarded as conditional on correct moral behavior.) But they are not necessarily associated. The religious practices of a society may encourage particular kinds of behavior without associating these with any particular reward. Take, for instance, the practice of declaring certain objects, persons, or actions as *tapu*. Rules regarding what is *tapu* come with threatened sanctions for violation, but offer no reward in the case of observance.

The term "normative" should be understood, in this context, in a broad sense. My category of the "normative" is broader than that of the "moral" or "ethical." Our notion of the ethical is that of universally binding norms that are associated with justice, fairness, and reciprocity. When I speak of normative claims, I mean only claims relating to how individuals ought to behave. Normative prescriptions, in this sense, need not be based on any general principle. Take, once again, rules regarding what is *tapu*. In Māori society, a chief (*rangatira*) could render a path *tapu* (Best 1982: 19), for no reason other than that he wanted it for his exclusive use. Unlike moral norms, the restriction thus created could also be temporary, for the *tapu* in question could be lifted, by a further ritual action (Best 1982: 28).

3.2 Small-Scale Societies

What are the goals sought by religious practices and traditional knowledge in small-scale societies?

3.2.1 Well-Being Goals

In the diffused religions of small-scale societies, the gods tend to have specialized roles, being gods of agriculture, fishing, warfare, and so on. Scholars have sometimes referred to these as "departmental gods," each having his or her own particular field of activity. The religious rituals directed to such gods tend to have this-worldly, tangible goals: "to procure food, ensure fine weather, and promote the health of the people and the welfare of the land" (Firth 1957: 34). Among the Māori people, for instance, the planting of *kumara* (sweet potato) was initiated and accompanied by prayers to various spiritual beings (*atua*), and the task was completed with "a ritual chant directed towards Rongo [*Rongo-hīrea*], the god of the *kumara*," with a view to ensuring a good harvest (Firth 1959: 266). When as religious practices are undertaken with a view to such this-worldly, practical benefits, they are practically indistinguishable from what is sometimes called "magic." (The Māori term *karakia* is commonly translated as "prayer," but can also be translated as "incantation" or even "spell.")

What about traditional knowledge regarding the natural world? What goals does it have? The acquisition of some such knowledge may be motivated by simple curiosity. The creation of etiological tales, for instance, may be motivated by nothing more than a desire to have some account of how the present order came to be. But (as we shall see shortly) such tales can also have a normative function, indicating how one ought to behave. The goals of other forms of traditional knowledge – those having to do with the classification and character of living things and practical know-how – are (like those of the corresponding religious practices) this-worldly and tangible. Indeed religious rituals and practical know-how are often regarded as complementary means of achieving the same ends. These shared this-worldly goals can be both individual and communal. It may be the whole community that is both praying and working for a successful harvest, or it may be individuals who are casting spells to attract a partner as well as adopting more tangible means of wooing the man or woman to whom they are attracted.

3.2.2 Normative Goals

What about normative goals? The question of whether the diffused religions of small-scale societies have normative goals is contested. Some scholars have noted that belief in moralizing high gods is characteristic only of large, complex societies, the gods of small-scale societies being less concerned with the enforcement of norms (Norenzayan 2013: 127–8, 132). It is true that the gods venerated in small-scale societies tend to be poor guides to correct conduct, sometimes engaging in activities of which the society itself would disapprove. Trickster gods, for instance, are unpredictable and can be positively mischievous. But even these gods can urge their followers to act in particular ways. Humans may be expected, for instance, to acknowledge "departmental" gods before taking resources for their own use. Among the Māori, for instance, it was the practice before felling a valuable tree to kindle sacred fires "to placate Tane and other gods, whose realm the forest is" (Best 1976: 322).

We should not, however, focus merely on gods. There are other religious practices within small-scale societies that play a normative role, helping to shape behavior. One of these is the narration and reenactment of myths: stories of a foundational era when the gods or ancestors established certain practices or institutions. Myths, in the sense of etiological tales, have a number of functions. But one of these is that of outlining how things ought to be. Myths can perform this function not just by telling stories – stories that "have a moral" (as we say) – but also by explaining how the institutions of society were established by ancestral figures.

Perhaps the clearest example of such myths are those that make up what is known as "the Dreaming," a translation of the term *alcheringa*, used by the Northern Arunta people of Australia. The stories that make up the Dreaming are accounts of the creation of the present order of things by mythic beings. But they are much more than this (Stanner 1972: 274). They justify social customs, the kinship system, and totemic categories, as well as the distribution of land and the existence of sacred sites. Even today, stories from the Dreaming can be used to encourage certain kinds of correct behavior (Klapproth 2004: 71–6).

Such myths commonly highlight the close relation between human beings and the natural world. In Māori thought, features of that world were associated with ancestors (*tūpuna*) (Smith 2000: 48). Elsdon Best (1856–1931), a forestry worker turned ethnographer, reported that when he was felling a tree, Māori would say to him: "*Kei te raweke koe i tō tipuna a Tane* (You are meddling with your ancestor Tane)" (Best 1982: 202). The origin of this saying is a creation myth that depicts Tane as the god of forests. This sense of relatedness to the natural world could even be expressed as an identification, as in a recent remark by a Māori elder, Turama Thomas Hawira. Speaking of his people's river that had become polluted, he said:

> It was with great sadness that we observed dead *tuna* [eels] and trout along the banks of our *awa tupua* [ancestral river]. ... Our river is stagnant and

dying. . . . *Ko au te awa, ko te awa ko au. Kei te mate te awa, kei te mate ahau.*
[I am the river and the river is me. If the river is dying, then so am I.]
(Salmond 2017: 300, 414)

These remarks contributed to a legal ruling that gave the river the legal status of a person, the local people being its spokesperson.

I have already noted the role of *tapu* in enforcing social norms. While this term is of Polynesian origin, it refers to practices that are much more widely distributed: practices of ritual avoidance and ritual prohibition. A ritual prohibition is a rule of behavior, the infringement of which is thought to bring about consequences for the offender. There are various conceptions of what these consequences will be, but they normally involve some kind of misfortune. The misfortune is commonly attributed to other-worldly powers, so that it can be averted only by the employment of the correct ritual.

Such broadly religious practices play variety of roles. They reinforce social norms, protect environmental resources from overuse, and establish property rights (Firth 1959: 246–53), as well as protecting individuals and the community from forces thought to be dangerous. Once again, some of the goals served by this practice overlap those served by traditional knowledge. Among Māori, the making of a fishing net involved not just practical skills and knowledge, but also the imposing of a *tapu* on the net, the workers, and the surrounding area. This "had the effect of keeping the energies of the people concentrated on their task, as well as of ensuring that strangers should not interfere" (Firth 1959: 248).

So much for the goals of diffused religion. But what about traditional knowledge? It clearly has practical goals, to do with very tangible forms of individual and communal well-being. But does it share normative goals with religion? Unlike modern science it does, although these normative goals are differently expressed, depending on the kind of traditional knowledge in question.

I suggested earlier that traditional knowledge takes four forms: (a) the classification of natural objects, (b) etiological tales associated with such objects, (c) beliefs about the properties of objects, and (d) practical know-how. Etiological tales (such as those of the Dreaming) commonly overlap the domain of religion, insofar as they are stories about gods or superhuman beings. We have seen that such stories not only "explain" features of the natural world; they also have the normative role of indicating how we should be related to it. Beliefs about the properties of objects may also have normative implications. They may specify, for instance, how a hunter should behave towards prey (Descola 2013: 3–4) or (as we have seen) how the feller of a tree should behave towards the forest (Best 1976: 322). Practical know-how seems a less likely candidate. It appears to have a normative dimension only insofar as any practical reasoning involves a conditional "ought." ("If you want your canoe to sail well, this is how you ought to build it.") Classificatory schemes might also appear to lack a normative role. But even they can function as a guide to action.

That last point is worth noting. One difference between the classificatory schemes of small-scale societies and those of modern science is that the former are (often, at least) immediately related to practical concerns. Traditional knowledge does offer some all-purpose categories. But it tends towards "special-purpose kinds," such as "poisonous mushrooms," which are related to particular human purposes (Ludwig 2018b: 33–4). It also offers more specific "recipes for action," such as "eating *green* apples may make you sick," or "harvest only the *largest males*" (Hunn 1982: 833). Scientific classifications, by way of contrast, abstract from such immediate human interests (Atran 1998: 563). Insofar as traditional classificatory schemes are already directed towards practical purposes, they can serve as a guide to action.

3.3 An Integral Cosmology

When it comes to the developed theoretical systems of literate cultures, I have suggested a distinction between an *integral* cosmology, such as that found in ancient China and an *integrated* natural philosophy, such as that found in medieval Europe. Both, in turn, can be distinguished from the compartmentalized science that is characteristic of European modernity.

3.3.1 The Goals of an Integral Cosmology

A key feature of the integral cosmology of ancient China is that it has normative (action-guiding) as well as speculative goals. Those who live in such a cosmos "know not only what is but what should be" (Graham 1989: 350). To put this in terms that have bedeviled modern Western philosophy, this cosmology knew of no split between "is" and "ought" (Peterson 1980: 29). Insofar as Chinese cosmology has a normative as well as a descriptive role, it fulfils one of the aims of religion. It does so, at least sometimes, without any reference to gods or a non-natural realm.

One illustration of this is the use of *yīnyáng* theory in the *Zhōulǐ* (*Chou-li*; *The Rites of Zhou*), which is one of the thirteen Confucian classics. Here the political structures of the state are arranged according to the principles of *yīn* and *yáng*, as are the differing varieties of teaching, and the various categories of ritual action (Wang 2012: 96–100). Such arrangements were often linked with the idea that the behavior of the ruler had cosmic consequences. We find this in the *Huáinánzi*, compiled in the second century BCE. Here we read, for instance, that the springtime growth of plants is dependent on the ruler's acting in the manner appropriate to the season, that is to say benevolently. If the ruler acts severely at that time, the growth of plants will be hindered (Major 1993: 31).

In such discussions, *yīnyáng* cosmology is coupled with the theory of the five elemental phases (*wǔxíng*) – wood, earth, fire, metal, and water – which were also used to explain a wide range of phenomena. Once again, they did so in ways that offered moral guidance. The idea of the *wǔxíng* played a particular role in the political disputes of the period of the former Han Dynasty, which were cast in terms of their proper sequence. We see this in the *Wǔxíng Zhì* (Treatise on the Five Phases), a document that forms part of the *Hànshū* (*Ch'ien Han shu*), the history of the former Han Dynasty. The traditional cycle of phases had been what is called a "conquest" cycle, in which earth is conquered by wood, wood by metal, metal by fire, and fire by water. That cycle had been used by the emperor of Qin (Ch'in) to legitimate the succession of his empire to that of the Zhou (Chou). Many Han scholars, however, disapproved of what they regarded as the despotism of the Qin emperor. This led the compilers of the *Wǔxíng Zhì* to replace the traditional sequence with another: a "generation cycle" of wood, fire, earth, metal, and water. This entailed a rejection of rule by violence, "substituting birth and nurturing for violence" (Wang 2000: 152).

The normative use of cosmological principles was not restricted to the political realm; it extended to ethical questions more generally. Teachings on gender relations, for instance, were also shaped by the perceived relation of *yīn* and *yáng*. A striking example can be found in the Daoist work, the *Tàipíngjīng* (*T'ai-p'ing Ching*; *Classic of Great Peace*). Although it comes from a slightly later period – that of the later (eastern) Han dynasty (25–220 CE) – it uses the principles of this integral cosmology to oppose female infanticide. Its argument is that maltreatment or killing of females damages the *qì* of the *yīn* principle. Since women correspond to earth, both embodying *yīn*, female infanticide has cosmic consequences. When infanticide is widely practiced "disasters will be plentiful" and "the world will not be at peace" (Wang 2012: 104).

3.3.2 The Goals of Religion

While the correlative cosmology of ancient China was broadly naturalistic, it made no clear distinction between science and religion. It had, as we have seen, religious elements and its goals overlapped those of religion. But this correlative cosmology was developed by a literate élite, while the practice of religion went well beyond its boundaries. So we can cast our gaze more broadly and ask what goals were pursued by the religious practices of this wider Chinese society.

We can begin with normative goals. The dominant moral norms of ancient Chinese society were not drawn from religion. The ethical norms of ancient

China were either traditional or emerged from the writings of the philosophers, particularly the Confucians. As one author puts it, Chinese religion was not "the fountainhead of moral ideas," but a way of "inducing the gods or spirits to bring happiness to man" (Yang 1961: 279). To this extent the religious practices of ancient China had much in common with the "diffused religion" of small-scale societies. Particular gods could be appealed to for particular practical purposes: "to ward off evil, to cure sickness, to obtain rain in a drought, to achieve victory in war and peace in a crisis" (Yang 1961: 279).

Yet even if religious practices are not the source of moral norms, they can contribute to enforcing them. So it was in ancient China. There were two main areas in which Chinese religious practices could shape behavior.

The first had to do with the safeguarding of family life. The practices linking religion to family life took two forms. First, there were the deities venerated within the home, to ensure the family's protection and well-being (Yang 1961: 28–9). Second, there was the veneration of ancestors, which involved both mortuary rites following the death of a family member and sacrificial rites to maintain the family's connection with those who had died (Yang 1961: 30–1). The practice of venerating ancestors also had practical as well as ethical goals. While for Confucians it embodied the proper attitude of filial piety, ancestors were commonly thought to watch over human conduct and confer this-worldly benefits (Barnwell 2013: 19–20).

A second area in which religious practices sought to shape behavior had to do with the state. The structure of the supernatural world was often depicted on the model of the imperial court in ways that helped to legitimate earthly power (Yang 1961: 144). Emperors were thought to enjoy the "mandate of Heaven" (*tiānmíng*) and headed a vast system of official religious practices. Both the Qin and Han emperors recognized and funded cultic practices that were then administered by local officials responsible to the emperor (Bujard 2009: 782–90). While these official cults were never exclusive – they existed alongside unofficial ones – they formed a network of religious practices that bound society together and helped to reinforce imperial authority.

3.4 Institutional Religions

In European history, the emergence of distinct religious communities – what I have called "institutional" rather than "diffused" religion – went hand-in-hand with a distinction between religious knowledge and knowledge of the natural world. The latter also involved a growing distinction between theoretical and normative aims. But this distinction was differently made at differing points in history, leading to differing conceptions of the relation between science and religion.

3.4.1 Patristic and Early Medieval Christianity

When Christian writers of the patristic and early medieval periods studied the natural world, they did so in ways that subordinated secular knowledge to religious goals. The subjects taught in monastic schools, for instance, were classified into what had been known since Roman times as the seven "liberal arts." These were the elementary studies of the *trivium* – grammar, rhetoric, and dialectic (the last being what we call "logic") – and the more advanced studies of the *quadrivium*, namely geometry, arithmetic, astronomy, and harmonics (musical theory). The teaching of these subjects did preserve some of the learning of the ancient world, but it was preserved "only insofar as it contributed to religious ends" (Lindberg 2007: 155). The liberal arts were valued as steps on the path to a higher wisdom, as aids to the interpretation of sacred scripture, or for their practical uses (Alberi 2001: 901). Astronomy, for instance, had a special place because of its importance for the church calendar.

Other than the study of astronomy, natural philosophy played a very minor role in the monastic curriculum. The monks did, however, preserve another way of understanding the natural world. Early Christian writers had regarded nature as a grand book, which – like sacred scripture itself – was written by God, and from which moral and religious lessons may be learned (Gregory 1966: 27–35). This led them to what we may call a *symbolic* understanding of nature, which attached moral and religious meanings to natural objects. Striking examples are to be found in the ancient Christian work known as the *Physiologus*, which was widely read by medieval Christians. Take, for instance, the hedgehog. "The hedgehog does not quite have the appearance of a ball," we read,

> as he is full of quills. . . . he climbs up to the grape on the vine and then throws down the berries (that is, the grapes) onto the ground. Then he rolls himself over on them, fastening the fruit of the vine to his quills, and carries it off to his young and discards the plucked stalk. And you, O Christian, refrain from busying yourself about everything and stand watch over your spiritual vineyard from which you stock your spiritual cellar. (Curley 1979: 24)

On this view of the natural world, all creatures, no matter how humble, can function as a mirror, in which the pious observer can glimpse messages from their creator (Gregory 1966: 28).

The cathedral schools established in the newly emerging cities of medieval Europe also taught the liberal arts: the subjects of the *trivium* and *quadrivium*. Here, too, such studies were thought to be of value insofar as they served a higher goal. But in this case, the goal tended to be ethical rather than directly religious. The cathedral schools commonly described their task as the teaching of *litterae et mores*, "letters and manners." But although this humanistic education had an ethical goal, it did not involve the teaching of ethics as a separate subject. The learning of ethical lessons was thought to emerge from the study of subjects such as grammar and rhetoric (Jaeger 1987: 576, 581).

3.4.2 Natural Philosophy and Religion

Clear distinctions between natural philosophy, theology, and ethics emerge (as we have seen) only in the later medieval period. Medieval thinkers regarded natural philosophy as part of a broader project, whose aims included a study of things divine and how we ought to live. While natural philosophy had its own methods and purposes, it could contribute to those religious and normative goals.

Aristotelian natural philosophy could contribute to normative goals because it made no pretense to being "value-neutral." It saw the world as a hierarchy of beings, each of which is moved by what is good, the ultimate good being the unmoved mover (Lloyd 1968: 295). This meant that the idea of value is built into Aristotelian science. Here, too, as in China, a distinction between "is" and "ought" makes little sense. Yet medieval natural philosophy differed from the integral cosmology of ancient China in distinguishing descriptive and normative goals. Philosophy had both kinds of goal, but pursued them in differing ways and by means of different disciplines.

In the late medieval universities, the old divisions of knowledge into the *trivium* and *quadrivium* gradually gave way to the Aristotelian classifications (Luscombe 2011: 27). As I noted in the previous section, these divided the sciences into the productive, the theoretical, and the practical. The *productive* sciences were immediately oriented to action. They included ship-building, agriculture, and medicine, as well as music, theatre, dance, and rhetoric. The *theoretical* sciences were primarily descriptive. They included mathematics, metaphysics, physics (the study of the general principles underlying the world of change), and special sciences such as biology and astronomy. The *practical* sciences were those with expressly normative concerns, having to do with what "ought to be" the case. They included politics and ethics, the sciences of correct individual and collective behavior. In a similar way, the study of things divine – "theology" in its pre-Christian sense – was distinguished from other forms of inquiry. It was distinguished, in particular, from the study of changing things, which belonged to physics and the special sciences.

I have emphasized these distinctions because some recent historians are inclined to overlook them. They claim that "the whole point of natural philosophy" was to see "the world as created by God" (Cunningham & Williams 1993:

421) or that "the study of nature" had as its primary purpose the ascent of the mind to divine truths (Harrison 2015: 71). This is a more accurate description of the program of the monastic schools than that of the universities. By the later medieval period, natural philosophy had come to have "its own proper field of rationality and legitimacy" (Biard 2001: 78) and its immediate aims were not identical with those of either ethics or religion. This partial autonomy of natural philosophy was aided by its institutional setting, as we shall see shortly.

3.4.3 Religion and Modern Science

What about modern science? At least on a noninstrumentalist view – one that sees science as aiming at truth rather than (merely) successful prediction – the sciences can be said to share a cognitive goal with religion. They, too, seek to tell us about aspects of the world, even those that are not immediately accessible to observation. But modern science differs from medieval natural philosophy in defining its goals more narrowly,

The medieval intellectual world was characterized by a clear distinction between the thinker and the artisan. What Aristotle called productive knowledge was distinguished from theoretical knowledge and the activities to which each referred were carried out by different people (Anstey & Vanzo 2012: 505). (This was also, it should be noted, true of China, where a similar divide developed between technical expertise and theoretical thought (Kim 1982: 91–2).) With the beginnings of modern science, three developments occurred. The first was a reconfiguring of the domains of knowledge, which blurred the distinction between theoretical and productive knowledge (the latter being the kind of knowledge possessed by the artisan). The second development was a rethinking of the aims of natural philosophy, which were defined in terms of just one aspect of productive knowledge, namely control over the natural world. The third development was a deepening divide between theoretical and productive knowledge, on the one hand, and ethical reflection, on other. This led to our modern distinction between "is" and "ought," between "facts" and "values."

All these developments are evident in the work of Francis Bacon (1561–1626). Before Bacon's time, there had been some apparent exceptions to the divide between theoretical and productive knowledge. Practitioners of the occult sciences, such as alchemy, had long sought to produce useful effects by tapping into the hidden ("occult") properties of nature. But while such hidden properties could be known by experience, they were thought to lie outside the scope of theoretical explanation (Hutchison 1982: 235–42). To this extent their scientific status was questionable. Roger Bacon (1215–92) – Francis's medieval namesake – had also argued for the development of an "experiential science" (*scientia experimentalis*), which would be of practical value. But he remained a medieval thinker insofar as he did not divorce such a science from ethical and religious concerns. Indeed, his *scientia experimentalis* includes insights gained by divine illumination, which have to do with moral virtues as well as the principles underlying the natural world (Bacon 1962: 585–6).

It is in the work of Francis Bacon that we see the first outlines of our modern conception of the scope of science. Bacon not only included the productive practices of magic within the scope of natural philosophy (Anstey & Vanzo 2012: 509); he also insisted that any form of natural philosophy should be judged by its practical utility. "The end [goal] which this science of mine proposes," he wrote, "is the invention not of arguments but of arts," that is to say, practical skills (Bacon 1989: 21). Bacon also insisted on a sharp separation between the realm of science and that of both ethics and religion. Appealing to the story of Adam and Eve, Bacon noted that the fall had entailed both a loss of dominion over the natural world and a loss of moral innocence. Natural philosophy, properly pursued, could restore humanity's dominion over nature. But it was left to religion to restore humanity's lost innocence (Bacon 2000: 221). This involved "a clear separation of natural knowledge and moral know-ledge" (Leiss 1974: 52).

Bacon did believe that the natural philosopher ought to have certain moral qualities. But whatever moral qualities natural philosophers were thought to possess, their work was no longer associated with the search for moral wisdom. The moral qualities of the natural philosopher pertained to the study of nature, not to the teaching of morality (Gaukroger 2001: 112). This disconnect was (as we shall see) reinforced by the development of scientific societies, distinct from the university faculties in which philosophy was taught. Did this mean that science itself was value-free, that it had no ethical dimension? No, it did not. It meant merely that scientists were cut off from the task of ethical reflection. This may have contributed to their becoming blind to the normative assumptions underlying their own enterprise.

What were those assumptions? The idea that the natural philosopher ought to have certain moral qualities has not played a prominent role in the history of modern science. But the values that Bacon believed should shape scientific inquiry have. Those values had to do with the appropriate relation of human beings and the natural world, which was thought to be one of domination and control. We see this in the work of another pioneer of modern science, Robert Boyle (1627–91). "Some men," Boyle writes, "care only to know nature, others desire to command her" (Boyle 1772: 310). It was the latter attitude that Boyle was advocating: one that sought not merely to understand nature, but to exploit it to meet human needs. Noteworthy, too, is Boyle's attack on those who would regard nature as a goddess, having agency and powers of her own. This attitude, he complains, stands in the way of human dominion over the natural world (Boyle 1996: 15 [sect. 1]). Nature should be seen as a passive entity, open to our exploitation.

The seventeenth-century divorce between natural philosophy and moral reflection had a further consequence. As science became the paradigmatic instance of knowledge and religion lost its taken-for-granted authority, moral knowledge also gradually lost its status. By the late eighteenth century, philosophers were already beginning to deny the existence of mind-independent moral facts, regarding moral obligations as simply a matter of "sentiment" or "feeling." On this view, it is science that tells us the facts about the world; moral inquiry tells us how human beings respond to those facts (Hume 1978: 469 [3.1.1]). The reader may agree with this view, for it is still widely defended. But whether or not we accept it, we should be aware of its historical roots.

4 The Organizational Dimension

I have discussed the cognitive dimension of the science and religion relation. I have outlined the development (particularly in European thought) of a clear distinction between scientific and religious beliefs, leading to the possibility of a perceived conflict between the two. I have also discussed the teleological dimension. Here we saw the gradual divorce of fact and value in the history of Western thought, leading to the idea that the goals of science are purely cognitive. It is time to examine the third dimension of the relation between *scientia* and religion. This is its *organizational* dimension, which has to do with the social institutions within which scientific and religious practices are embedded.

4.1 No Organizational Distinction

We may begin with a broad distinction: that between societies in which scientific and religious practices are carried out within different organizations and those in which they are not. It is the first of these that I shall spend most time discussing. But let me begin with the second: societies in which there is no such distinction.

4.1.1 Small-Scale Societies

As we have seen, small-scale societies – those characterized by hunting and gathering or subsistence agriculture – have both religious practices and bodies of knowledge about the natural world. But neither is institutionalized in the sense of having an organized body of interpreters and expert practitioners (Evans-Pritchard 1976: 205). There are expert practitioners in both domains.

African societies, for instance, have "medicine men" (*waganga* in Swahili), mediums, diviners, and rainmakers (Mbiti 1969: 166–93). But these specialists are individuals, who form (at most) loose associations (Evans-Pritchard 1976: 186). What unites them is that they have received a particular initiation into a body of knowledge, one to which other people are often denied access.

That initiation often *is* institutionalized. Among the peoples of the Gilbert Island (Kiribati), for instance, the training of navigators was an arduous process that could last many years. It involved (among other things) the memorization of the movements of sun, moon, stars, and planets, which were imaginatively projected onto the roof beams of a thatched hut in which the trainee navigator sat (Grimble 1972: 215–17). The Māori people also had an institutionalized way of passing on knowledge, namely "the house of learning" (*te whare wānanga*). The culturally significant knowledge transmitted by the *whare wānanga* was given only to certain young men, chosen partly for their powers of memory. Less culturally significant forms of knowledge were taught informally, often by a man to his son or grandson (Best 1923: 15, 27). Among Australian Aboriginal peoples, it was the initiatory rites for young men that provided the context for the transmission of tribal lore. Alongside what the "visible marks" of initiation – tooth removal, circumcision, or scarification – the initiates received "invisible marks" in the form of altered characters and the possession of secret knowledge (Maddock 1974: 142–3).

Although such institutions existed, they did not divide neatly into "scientific" and "religious." Some were relatively specialized, in the case of the teaching of navigational techniques. But even here the knowledge passed on dealt with both religious matters and knowledge of the natural world, the two being intertwined. The African *waganga* ("medicine man"), for instance, needed to be familiar with the medicinal value of natural objects (such as herbs, roots, leaves) as well as techniques for combating witchcraft (Mbiti 1969: 167–8). Even apparently secular knowledge, such as that relating to navigation, was sometimes conveyed by means of myths having a religious dimension. So while there are distinctions here, they do not correspond to our modern ones. Such institutions transmitted knowledge that we would think of as both scientific and religious.

4.1.2 An Integral Cosmology

What about the case of an integral cosmology, such as that found in ancient China? If we assume that this cosmology was functionally equivalent to what we call "science," did it involve an organizational distinction between practitioners of *scientia* and those of religion?

Later Chinese history saw the growth of distinctively religious communities – particularly Daoist and Buddhist – in which religious authority was institutionalized.

These distinctively religious groups entered into relations with nonreligious organizations, relations that were not always peaceful (Yang 1961: 301–3). But this had not been the case in earlier times, when the integral cosmology of ancient China was developing. During this period, there were certainly ritual specialists, just as there were those who had established roles within ritual practices (particularly in the imperial courts). But these roles existed within a religion that remained a diffused religion, that is to say, one embedded in social institutions it had not itself created (Yang 1961: 296–300).

If there were no organizations devoted to religion, were there organizations devoted to *scientia*? The closest one comes in ancient China to an organization devoted to reflection on the natural world is the class of people known as *shì* (*shih*). This term originally meant a noble person entitled to bear arms ("knight"), but it came to be applied to those who supported themselves by tasks that required literacy (Lloyd & Sivin 2002: 17). The earliest members of this group to focus on the natural world were the specialists in *shǔshù fāngjì*, "calculations and recipes": skills relating to divination, rituals, astronomy and astrology, calendar-making, music, and medicine.

While such practitioners existed, they did not seem to have regarded themselves as engaged in a common intellectual enterprise (Harper 1999: 817–18). A sense of collective identity emerged only among a particular group within the *shì*, who came to be known as *rú* (*ju*). While sometimes used for the followers of Confucius, the word *rú* also had a wider sense of "scholars" or "learned men", a group also known as the *bóshì* (*po-shih*), "the erudite" (Lloyd & Sivin 2002: 23, 27). When these scholars turned their attention to the nature of the world and the behavior of human beings, they did think of themselves as engaged in a common intellectual task. We know this from their disagreements with one another. Since that common task resembles what the Greeks called "philosophy," we commonly refer to these thinkers as "philosophers."

Not all early Chinese philosophers were sympathetic to the evolving cosmology of this period. Some, in particular the followers of Mòzĭ, ignored or were hostile to it (Graham 1989: 327). Neither did they invent its principles, which were developed by the specialists in *shǔshù fāngjì* (Harper 1999: 845). But it was philosophers who synthesized these principles and turned them into a more or less coherent worldview. The thinker traditionally credited with beginning this synthesis was Zōu Yăn (Tsou Yen; 305–240 BCE). Zōu Yăn's aims seem to have been more ethical and political than "scientific" in our modern sense. But (as we have seen) this is also true of the cosmology to which his work contributed, which found fuller expression in later thinkers, such as Dŏng Zhòngshū,

Before the establishment of the Han dynasty, such thinkers had to depend on the patronage of local rulers, who competed with one another in "building collections of clever, dangerous, or otherwise useful people" (Lloyd & Sivin 2002: 31). By the second century BCE, scholars were not solely dependent on patronage, but could find regular employment in the emerging Han bureaucracy (Sivin 1995: 20). But at least before the establishment of an "imperial academy" – the *tàixué (t'ai-hsüeh)*, literally "grand school" – in 124 BCE, this community of scholars had no institution of its own. Historians commonly speak of a "Jixia Academy" (*jìxià xuégōng [chi-hsia hsüeh-kung]*) founded about 381 BCE in the state of Qi, one of the major kingdoms of the period. But this gathering may have been nothing more than another instance of imperial patronage (Sivin 1995: 19–28).

What relation had this loose-knit community of thinkers to the practitioners of religion? Insofar as the class of those who led religious rituals was broader than that of the philosophers, we can speak of a distinction between philosophical and religious practitioners in ancient China. There were geomancers and diviners, shamans and sorcerers who were not *rú* (or even *shì*), for the religion of the literate élite was not the only form of religion in China (Harper 1999: 817). But there was also a significant overlap between the two groups. Correct ritual practice required knowledge of a kind that scholars claimed to be able to provide (Bujard 2009: 778). So it is not surprising to find that during the former Han dynasty, the term "erudite" (*bóshì*) was employed not only for teachers but also for ritual specialists (Sivin 1995: 25). Confucian thinkers in particular encouraged and practiced rituals of all kinds, including religious. So philosophers may have been involved not merely in shaping and interpreting religious practices, but also in leading them. In such a context, it makes little sense to speak of distinct "scientific" and "religious" organizations.

4.2 Distinct Organizations

In the history of Western Europe, we find a very different set of organizational relations between practitioners of *scientia* and those of religion. There are two developments that contributed to this. The first is the emergence of universities in the thirteenth century. The second is the establishment of scientific societies in the seventeenth century, giving rise (in due course) to the scientific organizations with which we are familiar today.

4.2.1 Monastic Schools

Before the thirteenth century, medieval Europe had no dedicated institutions for the study of natural philosophy. Physics (in the sense of the study of *phusis*, "nature") was a recognized field of inquiry – Hugh of St. Victor (1096–1141) defined it as the study of "the causes of things in their effects and the effects from their causes" – but it was the subject of relatively little attention (Cadden 1995: 1–2). One reason for this was an absence of authoritative texts. But the other was the institutional setting of learning, which in the early medieval period was that of the monastic schools. While the monastic schools did teach the sciences of the *quadrivium* – geometry, arithmetic, astronomy, and harmonics – they did so because of the ways they could serve the faith. When the natural world was studied, it was often in a symbolic sense, for the moral and religious lessons it could teach. In this context, there was no organizational distinction between those who studied natural philosophy and those who reflected on religion. Both were undertaken in the same institutional setting.

4.2.2 The Rise of Universities

An organizational distinction between the practice of science and thinking about religion emerges only with the emergence of universities in the thirteenth century. There are two features of the late medieval universities that are important in this respect.

The first is that the universities were corporations under medieval law. It is tempting to think that the word "university" refers to the range of subjects studied, but that was not its original meaning. The Latin *universitas* was the equivalent of our term "corporation": a legal entity representing a particular body of practitioners (Huff 1993: 135). As corporations, the universities had a degree of autonomy – a limited degree, admittedly, but some – and the ability to conduct their own affairs.

The second development was the distinction within the universities between the faculties of arts and the faculties of theology. It was within the faculty of arts that natural philosophy was studied, establishing an institutional distinction between natural science and (revealed) religion. That distinction was reinforced by attempts to keep philosophers from encroaching on theological topics. As we have already seen, in 1272, the Faculty of Arts at the University of Paris forbade its scholars from discussing theological questions. This meant that those studying the natural world had to be wary when approaching questions about God.

4.2.3 The Emergence of Scientific Societies

The development of modern science went hand-in-hand with further changes in its organizational setting. Some early modern scientific work relied on the patronage of powerful rulers. Galileo, for instance, moved from a university post (at the University of Padua) to the court of Cosimo II de Medici (1590–1621), the grand duke of Tuscany. But the same period saw a desire to establish organizations dedicated to the pursuit of natural philosophy, a desire vividly expressed in Francis Bacon's utopian work *New Atlantis*. At the center of Bacon's ideal society is a research institute for science and technology, named "Solomon's House" or (in another biblical allusion) the "College of the Six Days' Work." It is hard not to be struck by the almost god-like status of the director of this institute, whose rare appearances seem "to stun the onlookers into an attitude of reverence and utter docility" (Leiss 1974: 66). Noteworthy, too, is the fact that this ideal "scientific research establishment exercises complete control over its own activities and maintains an element of independence vis-à-vis the rest of society" (Leiss 1974: 68). This includes an oath of secrecy. It is the scientists who decide which of their discoveries are to be revealed to the nation and which are not.

Bacon's *New Atlantis* was merely a dream. But the dream begins to become a reality with the creation of specialist scientific societies. Perhaps the best known are the Accademia dei Lincei (Academy of the Lynxes), founded in 1603, the Royal Society of England, founded in 1660, and the French Académie Royale des Sciences, founded in 1666. By the mid-eighteenth century, there existed a clear model of a "republic of science," whose members

> investigated nature and reported their findings to each other, . . . arranged those findings in a systematic manner and interpreted their meanings, . . . evaluated interpretations proposed by others and defended their own conclusions. (Donovan 1996: 27)

This republic of science found its institutional home in the scientific societies, with their increasingly specialized reports and journals.

Why was this further change important? The medieval universities, as we have seen, distinguished between the faculty of arts and that of theology, natural philosophy being undertaken within the faculty of arts. This meant it was part of a larger enterprise, for the faculty of arts was (as the University of Paris put it) a faculty of "rational, moral, and natural philosophy" (McLaughlin 1955: 197). The development of scientific societies severed this link, reinforcing the separation of scientific research from ethical and religious inquiry. This development was, perhaps, at its clearest in England, where the authority of the Royal Society was expressly limited to "matters philosophical, mathematical, and mechanical" (Sprat 1734: 142). Early modern natural philosophers were certainly motivated by ethical and religious beliefs. But within the newly founded scientific societies, the results of natural philosophical inquiry were not brought into dialogue with ethical and religious concerns. Not only were science and religion organizationally separated, as they had been in the medieval universities, but science and moral philosophy were also divorced.

5 The Epistemological Dimension

I have examined the cognitive, teleological, and organizational dimensions of the science and religion relation. This study has revealed two developments in the history of European societies, developments that did not occur elsewhere. The first was a clear distinction between science and religion as ways of understanding the world. The second was a gradual increase in the autonomy of scientific inquiry. It is time to turn to the final dimension of this inquiry, which is *epistemological*, having to do with conceptions of knowledge. There are three issues to be discussed here. The first has to do with the kinds of knowledge to which religions and the various forms of *scientia* lay claim. The second has to do with the ways in which these knowledge claims are expressed. A third issue has to do with the sources of this alleged knowledge: where do scientific and religious thinkers believe their ideas come from?

5.1 Knowing How and Knowing That

What kinds of knowledge do the sciences and religion claim to transmit? A useful distinction here is that between two forms of knowledge. Philosophers commonly distinguish these as *knowing how* and *knowing that*, while psychologists use a different terminology, speaking of *declarative* and *procedural* knowledge.

Although already implicit in the work of the Chinese philosopher Zhuāngzǐ (Chuang Tzǔ), who lived in the fourth century BCE (Watson 2013: 106–7), this distinction is more fully developed in an essay by the philosopher Gilbert Ryle, published in 1946. Alongside the kind of knowledge that involves assent to propositions, Ryle argued, there is a different kind of knowledge, which consists in the possession of a skill. The skills involved may be very different in character. Ryle's examples include cooking of an omelet, designing a dress, and persuading a jury (Ryle 1946: 8). But they have some features in common. In particular, "knowing how" commonly involves *tacit* knowledge: knowledge that is not articulated in words or reflected on. Even when it is articulated in words – when there are explicit rules and procedures to be learned – skilled performance requires practitioners to "internalize" this knowledge so that it no longer needs to be consciously recalled. Learning how to play a musical instrument is a familiar example of how one acquires knowledge of this kind.

There has been much discussion among philosophers about whether one of these forms of knowledge can be reduced to the other. Some argue that all instances of "knowing how" can be explained in terms of "knowing that." Others argue that all instances of "knowing that" can be explained in terms of "knowing how." Ignoring this debate, I shall simply assume that the distinction is a useful one.

5.1.1 Knowing How in Religion

Many philosophers take it for granted that the knowledge religions claim to offer is a "knowing that": a particular description of the way the world is. But the metaphysical claims made by religions are conditioned by their normative goals. Those normative goals, in turn, involve a certain kind of "knowing how," the knowledge of how to live a particular kind of life. Knowledge that does not contribute to this goal is often considered religiously worthless.

Take, for instance, the following story about the Buddha. A monk complains that he has not yet received the answers to certain important questions: whether the world is eternal or not eternal, whether it is infinite or finite, or whether the life principle is identical with the body or separate from it. How does the Buddha reply? "It is as if," he says,

> a man were struck by an arrow that was smeared thickly with poison; his friends and companions, his family and relatives would summon a doctor to see to the arrow. And the man might say, "I will not draw out this arrow as long as I do not know whether the man by whom I was struck was a brahmin, a *kúatriya*, a *vaiśya*, or a *śūdra* [the traditional classes of Vedic society] . . . as long as I do not know his name and his family . . . whether he was tall, short or of medium height . . . " That man would not discover these things, but that man would die. (Gethin 1998: 66)

This suggests that the Buddha had no interest in metaphysical questions for their own sake. As one scholar writes, "the knowledge that the Buddha was trying to convey is more akin to a skill, like 'knowing how' to play a musical instrument, than [to] a piece of information, such as what time the Manchester train leaves tomorrow" (Gethin 1998: 36). We should avoid setting this particular "knowing how" in opposition to a "knowing that." After all, the first step on the Buddhist eightfold path is adopting a "right view" of reality, which means accepting the four Noble Truths. But even if Buddhist "knowing how" also involves a "knowing that," the "knowing that" is considered significant only insofar as it contributes to the cultivation of something like a skill.

Some religions give particular weight to "knowing that": propositional knowledge about the nature of things. Christianity, in particular, insists on the importance of orthodoxy (correct belief), even about matters that may (at first sight) appear to have few practical effects. The doctrine of the trinitarian nature of God is a striking example. Even in these cases, however, correct belief is thought to be important because of its power to shape the lives of believers. When Orthodox theologians, for instance, argue against the Western church's version of the trinitarian doctrine, they do so on the grounds that it has deleterious effects, distorting our understanding of what it means to be saved (Iacovetti 2018: 74).

Other religions, by way of contrast, place relatively little stress on correct belief. Their emphasis is on what is sometimes called "orthopraxy," correct practice, both in the everyday behavior of individuals and the performance of rituals. Members of small-scale societies, for instance, certainly have stories about gods or ancestors and their interactions with humans. But (as we have seen) these are not developed into bodies of doctrine, neither are they considered sacred and unalterable (Mbiti 1969: 3). Members of small-scale societies may, however, place great emphasis on correct practice, particularly when it comes to ritual actions. Among Māori, for instance, it was not only important to preserve the proper form of a *karakia* (incantation); it needed to be recited without slip or error (Firth 1959: 270).

What I have called the "post-institutional" religion of our own age – that of loosely organized and informal groups – also tends to play down propositional in favor of skill-based knowledge. The knowledge that is valued in this context has to do with how to attain a state of well-being. Practitioners of Wicca (modern witchcraft), for instance, apparently believe their rituals are effective. But there is no single, orthodox account of what makes them effective. Neither do most practitioners have a fully worked out theory on this matter (Luhrmann 1989: 283). One becomes a member of such a group not by subscribing to a set of beliefs, but by learning how to take part in its practices (Luhrmann 1989: 312).

5.1.2 Knowing How in Traditional Knowledge

I suggested earlier that the traditional knowledge of small-scale societies is as much a manner of "being in the world" as it is a way of understanding it. This is another way of saying that it is as much a matter of "knowing how" as of "knowing that." Much of this knowledge is tacit knowledge, skill-based knowledge that practitioners may or may not be able to put into words. It is embodied knowledge, akin to what we often call "muscle memory," although developed to greater extent than is required in a culture such as ours, which depends on literacy and complex tools.

Once again, navigational knowledge provides a striking example. An important element of navigational skill among the inhabitants of the Marshall Islands is the ability to identify different kinds of wave, distinguishing (a) long-distance swells from (b) short, local waves and both of these from (c) waves that are reflected from some land mass. This knowledge was sometimes made explicit, particularly in what have become known as "stick charts," made by lashing thin strips of pandanus tree roots or coconut palms into a latticework pattern. In some cases, these do not represent actual wave patterns and actual islands; they appear to be abstract models of patterns and islands (Genz 2016: 19). Such models are, however, used only for learning. On the open sea, the navigator relies on memory and the ability to sense subtle changes in the movement of his canoe. That ability has been developed by long periods of training. One navigator, for instance, recalled that as a child he was placed

> blindfolded in a canoe while his grandfather towed him to various positions around a coral islet so that he could determine his location based on how the intersections and reflections of incoming waves from the ocean and lagoon affected the motion of the canoe. (Genz 2016: 13)

A training of this kind means that a navigator can sense subtleties of wave motion that he may not be able to put into words.

5.1.3 Knowing How in Science

What role does "knowing how" play within the various forms of *scientia*? One might argue that the correlative cosmology of ancient China, with its normative as well as descriptive goals, resembles religion in this respect. Its goal is knowing how to lead a certain kind of life. The natural philosophy of medieval Europe made a clearer distinction between descriptive and normative claims, as we have seen. But here, too, the study of the natural world was sometimes seen as part of a larger enterprise, the ultimate goal of which was to become a particular kind of person. William of Auvergne (1180–1249), for instance, wrote that the study of nature can lead to both "the exaltation of the creator and the perfection of our souls" (Harrison 2015: 69). But what I shall focus on here is modern science, where the role of "knowing how" is sometimes overlooked. While in the case of religion "knowing that" is subordinate to "knowing how," in the case of (modern) science the priority is reversed. Procedural knowledge is at the service of declarative knowledge. But while "knowing how" is at the service of "knowing that", it constitutes an important dimension of the practice of science.

One could argue that any process of discovery – scientific or otherwise – is guided by a tacit anticipation of its conclusion, such that certain lines of inquiry seem promising and others do not (Polanyi 2009: 21–4). Such an anticipation may be tacit in the sense that the researcher is unable to spell out what gives her this feeling. She just senses that this will be a profitable line of inquiry. The more skilled the researcher, the more likely it is that this intuitive sense will be reliable (Kahneman & Klein 2009: 520–3). It is true that this intuitive sense plays only a heuristic role: one that serves the process of discovery. Such intuitive anticipations must be tested, ideally experimentally. But experimental testing itself involves a wide range of skills: the scientist must learn how to observe and discriminate, to perform accurate measurements, to manipulate the experimental apparatus, and to interpret the resulting data. Successful experimental work requires "a feel for phenomena" (Kirschner 1992: 293), which can be gained only by practice.

5.2 Modes of Representation

There is a second kind of epistemological difference between science and religion, which has to do with their differing ways of representing the world. The discussion of these differences may be said to have begun with Aristotle's distinction between *mythos* and *logos*, to which I shall return in a moment. But they took on particular urgency with the development of anthropology, as ethnographers tried to understand the sometimes puzzling forms of expression found within small-scale societies. Famous examples include the claim made by the Bororo people of Brazil that they are "red parrots" and the assertion of the Nuer people of the southern Sudan that "twins are birds" (Smith 1972: 392, 405).

There is no reason to think these differences are innate, as though differing peoples had differing kinds of brain, leading them to represent the world in different ways. Differing modes of representation do build on innate features of the human mind, but they are culturally transmitted, being what an earlier generation of thinkers called "collective representations" (Durkheim 2010: 10). A variety of collective representations may be found within what we think of as a single culture, being employed in differing contexts. Within our own culture, for instance, a lay preacher who is also a scientist may employ one mode of representation in the laboratory and a very different one in the pulpit.

While these cultural forms begin life as "modes of representation," they eventually become "modes of thought," shaping our ways of conceiving what exists. The modern natural sciences, for instance, commonly employ mathematical models to represent the object of their study. While this way of representing the world makes possible precise predictions, it also makes certain aspects of our experience invisible (Husserl 1970: 60). Modern physics, for instance, not only ignores questions of value; its representations of the world also have no place for color, taste, and smell. The electromagnetic spectrum, for instance, represents features of the world that give rise to our experience of color. But a theory of electromagnetism will contain no terms referring to color. Color, along with other "secondary qualities," is thought to exist only when an observer interacts with the colorless, soundless, odorless, and valueless world described by physics (Galileo 1960: 311).

5.2.1 A Spectrum of Modes

Those who write about these differing modes of representation sometimes make sharp distinctions between them. Perhaps the best known example is Lucien

Lévy-Bruhl (1857–1939). In his early writings Lévy-Bruhl spoke about the "prelogical" mentality of small-scale societies (Lévy-Bruhl 1926: 78), while his later work made a contrast between "causal" and "participatory" orientations to the world (Lévy-Bruhl 1975: 92). Even more recent writers make sharp distinctions of this kind. Merlin Donald, for instance, distinguishes "mimetic" thought (which involves representations without language), from "mythic" thought (which involves narrative and metaphor), and both of these from "theoretic" thought (which operates by way of argument, discovery, and proof) (Donald 1991: 168, 214, 274).

While such distinctions are helpful, they can also be misleading. First of all, we may be tempted to turn them into a unilinear scheme of cultural evolution, as though all cultures were predestined, by a kind of internal necessity, to pass from one stage to the next. This way of thinking should be avoided. It merely judges other cultures against the particular history of our own and can lead to the idea that cultures that make extensive use of myth are somehow underdeveloped or "primitive." A second misunderstanding is to regard these categories as mutually exclusive, as though they could never be found together. This, too, would be a mistake. Even science, as we shall see in a moment, cannot entirely abandon mythic modes of representing the world.

For these reasons, it may be more helpful to see these different ways of representing reality as a falling on a spectrum. At one end of the spectrum are forms of speech that attempt to be as literal as possible and which employ carefully structured arguments. Such thinking distinguishes between different kinds of knowledge claim – religious, ethical, political, and scientific – and tries to keep them distinct. At the other end of the spectrum are forms of speech that use narrative rather than argument and are rich in imagery and metaphor.

Discourse of the latter kind often combines knowledge claims that we may regard as belonging to different categories. This is particularly the case in small-scale societies, where a "genealogy or narrative may explain the evolution of the world, [and] a poetic song or saying [may] teach tribal history" (McRae 2000: 1–2). In these societies, knowledge claims that we would think of as scientific and religious are interwoven. Astronomical knowledge, for instance, derived from careful observation, may be presented in religious terms, the heavenly bodies being regarded as gods (Best 1922: 64–5). Practical knowledge, such as that relating to navigation, may be embodied in what appear to be mythic narratives (Biggs 1994: 8). In nonliterate cultures, this embedding of natural knowledge within myth may serve as an aid to memory (Grimble 1972: 218). But it is also found in civilizations with a written literature. The Chinese classic, the *Huáinánzi*, for instance, contains precise astronomical knowledge within what appears to be a mythic account of the origin of the cosmos (Lloyd 1999: 150–1).

5.2.2 Science and Metaphor

In societies that make a distinction between science and religion, these differing modes of representation are more clearly distinguished. While religion remains bound to metaphor and myth, philosophy and the sciences strive for more literal forms of speech. Aristotle, for instance, was aware of the value of narrative and metaphor. He could even remark that "the lover of myth is in a sense a lover of wisdom" (Aristotle 1925: 12 [982b18]). But he also made a sharp distinction between philosophy and myth, contrasting "those who speak mythically" about the gods with those who employ "the language of proof" (Aristotle 1925: 128 [1000a18–20]). Late medieval thinkers also made distinctions between metaphorical and literal forms of speech, prompted in part by issues in biblical interpretation. Thomas Aquinas, for instance, insisted that while figurative interpretations of scripture were permissible, theological discussion should draw on the literal sense of the text (Aquinas 1969: 60 [1a 1.10]).

The modern sciences have inherited the philosophers' preference for literal forms of speech. The first historian of the Royal Society, Thomas Sprat (1635–1713), complained about the "Mists and Uncertainties" created by "specious Tropes and Figures." Avoiding such figurative language, he wrote, members of the Royal Society seek to return "to the primitive Purity and Shortness [of language], ... bringing all Things as near the mathematical Plainness as they can" (Sprat 1734: 112–13). While scientists writing popular works occasionally set out to create new myths, to compete with religious ones (Wilson 2004: 192), in their strictly scientific writings they eschew narrative and metaphor.

As in the case of scientific claims to value neutrality, we may doubt if this scientific ideal of "mathematical plainness" could ever be attained. Models, analogies, and metaphors remain important, even within science. Scientists may, for instance, employ metaphors to express theoretical claims without being able to offer any literal paraphrase (Boyd 1993: 486). Indeed the very idea of an entirely univocal language may itself be a chimera, an unreachable goal. "All language," it can be argued, "is metaphorical" (Hesse 1988). But whatever the practicality of the scientific ideal, it remains a sought-after goal. The sciences strive to eliminate the ambiguities characteristic of narrative and metaphorical modes of representation.

5.2.3 Religion and Metaphor

As a theoretical discipline, which aspires to be "scientific" in a broad sense, theology also attempts to eschew narrative and metaphor in favor of more literal modes of representation. But theology is bound to nonliteral forms of speech in ways that the sciences are not.

There are two reasons for this. The first is that a theology that appeals to an alleged divine revelation is bound to the texts in which that revelation is thought to be embodied. Such texts are commonly rich in narrative and metaphor. (Hence the need for a theological hermeneutics, setting out the principles by which scripture is to be interpreted.) A second reason has to do with the nature of theology's object, namely God. It is a commonplace of theological discourse that the nature of God exceeds human comprehension. If we can know anything of God, it can only be by way of metaphor or analogy (Aquinas 1969: 202–3 [1a 13.3]). This imposes limits to the theoretical precision that is possible when speaking of God. It is one of the reasons why theology cannot make experimentally testable predictions. To make precise predictions, one must be able to determine what would follow if a claim were true. But a metaphorical utterance has too many possible implications.

5.3 Sources of Knowledge

A final matter to be discussed has to do with what are believed to be the sources of religious and scientific claims to knowledge.

5.3.1 Sacred Knowledge

Many cultures have attributed their most valued forms of knowledge to a nonhuman, otherworldly source. Some Australian Aboriginal peoples, for instance, claim that their rock art (containing images of mythological figures) was not created by human beings, but dates from the time of the Dreaming (Maddock 1970: 449). Sometimes a conviction of this kind is extended to all varieties of knowledge. The Māori people distinguished three "baskets" (*kete*) of knowledge: the *kete tuauri* (basket of ancient knowledge), having to do with the gods, their genealogies, and human origins, the *kete tuatea* (basket of anxiety), which dealt with the knowledge of evil, and the *kete aronui* (basket of agreeable things), which dealt with practical and useful arts. While these represent different kinds of knowledge, they were all thought to have been obtained for humankind by the god Tane (Best 1923: 11).

Associated with this idea of a nonhuman origin was the fact that many kinds of knowledge were considered *tapu*, access to it being restricted. Among Australian Aboriginal peoples, for instance, certain kinds of information were made available only among those who shared certain kinship and totemic relations. Songs, stories, and knowledge of sacred places were often kept secret from women and uninitiated men (Klapproth 2004: 77–8). In Māori society, the place where the most *tapu* knowledge was transmitted – the *whare wānanga* – was itself considered *tapu*. Entry to it and exit from it involved rituals and no woman was permitted to participate (Best 1923: 16).

I have noted earlier that distinctions between *scientia* and religion are diffi-cult to make in small-scale societies. The attribution of apparently "natural" knowledge to a supernatural source is yet another illustration of this fact. But it is not just within small-scale, nonliterate societies that knowledge of the natural world has been regarded as having a divine origin. According to a widespread Chinese tradition, diagrams representing cosmological principles were revealed by heaven on the back of a dragon-like horse and a tortoise (Wang 2012: 208–12). An important instance of this idea in the history of Western thought is the doctrine of divine illumination. Inspired by the work of Plato, the followers of St. Augustine believed that the acquisition of some kinds of knowledge was possible only with divine assistance. In particular, they held that scientific knowledge required a greater-than-human source, a divine illumination.

Modern readers may be inclined to confuse this idea with another: that of a supernatural source of knowledge accessed by faith, which I shall discuss in a moment. The two resemble one another, insofar as they both involve a divine initiative. Religious faith requires a divine initiative supporting the act of faith, enabling us to accept certain propositions as divinely revealed. The doctrine of divine illumination also speaks of a divine initiative, but that initiative is more directly cognitive (Pasnau 2015: sect. 1). It holds that divine illumination is required for a number of apparently ordinary cognitive activities, which are engaged in by believers and nonbelievers alike.

While this doctrine has theological roots, it was motivated by two features of human knowledge. The first has to do with those principles of thought that appear to be necessarily true. These included mathematical truths, logical principles such as that of noncontradiction (that no statement of the form "p and not-p" can be true), and principles such as that of sufficient reason (that every contingent fact has a cause). While these appear to be essential to thought, it is difficult to see how we could arrive at them by observation. A second motivation was related to the Aristotelian ideal of science. Science was thought to involve a grasp of the essential properties of objects: that which makes them the kinds of objects they are. Advocates of divine illumination argued that we can do this only because God has "bathed" our minds (as it were) in his own, uncreated light. This allows us to understand the essences of created beings by reference to their exemplars in the mind of God.

Under the influence of Aristotle, late medieval thinkers came to reject this doctrine. Aquinas, for instance, holds that that while our capacity to know scientific truths has a divine origin, its exercise requires no special divine assist-ance (Aquinas 1972: 67–72 [1a2ae 109.1]). A more explicit rejection of the doctrine is to be found in the work of Duns Scotus (1266–1308). While believing that the human mind was created by God and owes all its powers to God, Scotus denied that scientific knowledge involved a special divine illumination (Dawes 2017: sect. 4.2). This marked a crucial step in the secularization of scientific knowledge. Our cognitive capabilities may be created by God, but their employment was no longer thought to require a special act of divine assistance.

5.3.2 Knowing by Faith

There remained, however, one kind of knowledge that religious thinkers believed to have a divine origin. This was the knowledge revealed by God and accessible only by faith. There are many conceptions of what it means to know something "by faith." The one I am describing here is a very common one, at least within Christian history, being spelled out most clearly in the work of Aquinas (Dawes 2015: 63–75). It sees faith as the divinely assisted act by which humans accept certain propositions as revealed by God. On this view, there is a clear distinction between faith and reason. "Reason" embraces that which we can know by means of our unaided cognitive faculties; "faith" is a form of knowledge by testimony. It includes matters we could never know by means of our native faculties, but which we come to know by means of a divine revelation. We accept this revelation by a decision, an act of the will, which is motivated by a love for God. Because this knowledge comes from God, we can be certain of its truth.

The problem with this conception of faith was highlighted by John Locke (1632–1704). If we ask how we know certain matters to be revealed by God, there are two options available. The first is to ask for evidence: what reason do we have to believe that a particular source of knowledge is divine? Why should we, for instance, regard Jesus as the embodiment of the divine word or the Qur'an as the uncreated speech of God? But this question throws us back on what our human powers can tell us. We have collapsed faith into reason and the alleged certainty of faith is undermined. Our confidence in what is thought to be revealed by God can be no greater than the force of the reasons we have for believing that this is a divine revelation and that we have understood it correctly (Locke 1829: 510 [4.16]).

Faced with this problem, believers commonly try to make the revelation of God "self-authenticating": it bears witness to itself (Calvin 1961: 80 [1.7.5]). Perhaps the clearest expression of this view is found in the Roman Catholic definition of faith produced by the first Vatican Council (1870):

> The Catholic Church declare faith to be a supernatural virtue by means of
> which we believe those things that have been revealed by him to be true, not
> on the basis of the intrinsic truth of the matter seen by the natural light of

reason, but on the authority of God himself revealing, who can neither deceive nor be deceived. (Denzinger & Schönmetzer 1976: 589 [§3008])

On this view, reliance on human reason for the certainty of faith is expressly excluded. It is God himself who assures us that what he is saying is true.

This makes the act of faith at least partially self-authenticating. Religious faith believes certain propositions on the authority of God on the authority of God. (This is not a typographical error.) The authority of God is simultaneously that which (*id quod*) and that by virtue of which (*id quo*) one believes (Hervé 1935: 350). I say *partially* self-authenticating because some theologians hold that reason can offer some independent support to the act of faith. But they also insist that a faith dependent on reason is not properly speaking *religious* faith (Dawes 2015: 66). If this view seems fatally question-begging to my readers, I can assure them they are not alone. (For a defense, see Stump 1989.) But whatever we make of it, it creates a sharp distinction between two sources of knowledge – divine revelation and human reason – and reinforces the possibility that they will at some time come into conflict.

6 Final Reflections

What this study has tried to highlight is the variety of ways in which science (as *scientia*) and religion have been related. As modern Western thinkers, we are inclined to make sharp distinctions. We think of science and religion as dealing with different matters and having differing goals. Scientific and religious practices are also embodied in distinct institutions, and employ very different ways of representing the world. But when placed in a wider cultural and historical context, our own society seems to be an outlier.

Small-scale societies, for instance, may have had no science, but they certainly had bodies of belief about the natural world. Insofar as these traced the origins of things to a mythic past, populated by gods and superhuman beings, these bodies of knowledge overlapped the domain of religion. Neither did such societies make clear distinctions between practical and theoretical knowledge. Even if their accounts of the natural world were sometimes motivated by sheer curiosity, for the most part this knowledge was local and applied. Mythic stories of origin also had a normative role, setting out and helping to shape what was thought to be appropriate behavior.

A similar combination of normative and descriptive goals characterized the integral cosmology developed in ancient China. What modern philosophers would consider a fallacy – deriving an "ought" from an "is" – would have appeared to be no fallacy at all to the philosophers of the Qin and Han dynasties.

Neither can one sharply distinguish science and religion in this context. While the Chinese cosmology was broadly naturalistic, it also had its religious elements, particularly in its conception of "heaven," which never entirely lost the features of a personal deity.

In the history of Western thought, it was Aristotle who began to make distinctions between various kinds of knowledge: the practical, the productive, and the theoretical. Normative questions, concerning how we are to live, fell within the realm of the practical sciences, while the theoretical sciences were further divided, into mathematics, metaphysics, physics, and various special sciences. This classification made for a distinction between normative and descriptive disciplines. This, however, was a distinction rather than a separation. Medieval philosophy kept these concerns together, insofar as they all lay within the scope of philosophical inquiry. The Faculty of Arts at the University of Paris was not restricted to what we call "the humanities"; it was a faculty of "rational, moral, and natural philosophy."

One aspect of the medieval universities did, however, foreshadow the later separation of science and religion. This was the distinction between the faculty of arts and the faculty of theology, the latter being devoted to a theology different in kind from that discussed by Aristotle. This theology went beyond what could be known of the divine by human reason, discussing matters that were thought to have been revealed by God, a knowledge derived not from reason but from faith. This leads to a clearer distinction between science and religion, as well as the possibility that the two may come into conflict.

This development continued with the rise of modern science. Here we see a further division emerging, not just between natural philosophy and (revealed) theology, but between the domain of science and that of normative inquiry. This separation was then institutionalized, with the founding of dedicated scientific societies, which studied the natural world but eschewed ethical reflection. The result was both a science shaped by normative assumptions of which its practitioners were unaware and a downgrading of the status of moral knowledge. Since science tried to avoid narrative and metaphor, these ways of representing the world were also downgraded. It was a purportedly value-free science, on this view, that told us what the world is really like.

I began this study with a sobering thought. It was that while we may regard small-scale societies as "primitive," many of them have survived for much longer periods of time than our own society has. Present indications are that their record will remain unbroken. We have seen that modern science has sought not merely to understand the world, but to reshape it. This attitude, coupled with the demands of a capitalist economy, may have brought us to the brink of civilizational collapse. Many of us will not regret the separation of scientific inquiry from religion, at least from the kind of religion that appeals to an authoritative divine revelation. But we may regret the separation of scientific inquiry from normative concerns that accompanied it. We may believe that alternative ways of regarding the natural world embodied truths that modern science has neglected.

What are those truths? Here's one suggestion. While the mythic thought of small-scale societies highlighted our dependence on the natural world, the integral cosmology of ancient China highlighted the natural world's dependence on our actions. The reasons both offered may be reasons we can no longer accept, but the truth to which they were pointing remains. When indigenous peoples speak of the earth-mother as a goddess, we may regard this as a metaphor. We may refuse to take literally the claim that "heaven" responds to human actions. But if these are metaphors, they are metaphors that convey truths. When Robert Boyle suggested we should not describe the earth as a goddess, he had lost sight of one of these truths. Happily it has been rediscovered by one of his scientific successors, who has drawn attention to our relationship to the earth by reviving the metaphor (Lovelock 2000: vii). Can we grasp and act on such truths before it is too late? That may be the most important question of our age.

References

Aikenhead, G. S. and M. Ogawa (2007). Indigenous Knowledge and Science Revisited. *Cultural Studies of Science Education* 2(3), 539–620.

Alberi, M. (2001). The Better Paths of Wisdom: Alcuin's Monastic "True Philosophy" and the Worldly Court. *Speculum* 76(4), 896–910.

al-Ghazālī, Abū Hāmid (2000). *The Incoherence of the Philosophers*, transl. Michael E. Marmura. Islamic Translation Series. Provo, UT: Brigham Young University Press.

Anstey, P. and A. Vanzo (2012). The Origins of Early Modern Experimental Philosophy. *Intellectual History Review* 22(4), 499–518.

Aquinas, T. (1969). *Summa theologiae*, vol. 1: The Existence of God, part 1: Questions 1–13, ed. Thomas Gilby. Garden City, NY: Image Books.

Aquinas, T. (1972). *Summa theologiae*, vol. 30 (1a2ae 106–114), trans. Cornelius Ernst. London: Blackfriars.

Aquinas, T. (1986). *The Division and Methods of the Sciences. Questions V and VI of his Commentary on the De Trinitate of Boethius*, transl. A. Maurer, 4th ed. Medieval Sources in Translation. Toronto: Pontifical Institute of Mediaeval Studies.

Aristotle (1925). *Metaphysics I–IX*, transl. H. Tredennick, Loeb Classical Library, Cambridge, MA: Harvard University Press, London: William Heinemann.

Astuti, R. and P. L. Harris (2008). Understanding Mortality and the Life of the Ancestors in Rural Madagascar. *Cognitive Science* 32(4), 713–40.

Atran, S. (1998). Folk Biology and the Anthropology of Science: Cognitive Universals and Cultural Particulars. *Behavioral and Brain Sciences* 21(4), 547–69.

Augustine (1982). *The Literal Meaning of Genesis*, vol. 1, transl. J. H. Taylor. Ancient Christian Writers 41. New York: Paulist Press.

Bacon, F. (1989). The Great Instauration (1620), in *New Atlantis and The Great Instauration*, ed. J. Weinberger, rev. ed. Arlington Heights, IL: Harlan Davidson, pp. 7–32.

Bacon, F. (2000). *The New Organon*, eds. L. Jardine and M. Silverthorne. Cambridge Texts in the History of Philosophy. Cambridge: Cambridge University Press.

Bacon, R. (1962). *The Opus Majus of Roger Bacon*, transl. R. B. Burke, vol. 2. New York: Russell & Russell.

Barbour, I. G. (1997). *Religion and Science: Historical and Contemporary Issues*. San Francisco, CA: HarperCollins.

Barnwell, S. A. (2013). The Evolution of the Concept of *De* 德 in Early China. *Sino-Platonic Papers* 235, 1–83.

Berlin, B. (1992). *Ethnobiological Classification: Principles of Categorization of Plants and Animals in Traditional Societies*. Princeton, NJ: Princeton Universal Press.

Best, E. (1922). *The Astronomical Knowledge of the Maori, Genuine and Empirical*. Dominion Museum Monograph 3. Wellington, New Zealand: Dominion Museum.

Best, E. (1923). *The Maori School of Learning: Its Objects, Methods, and Ceremonial*. Dominion Museum Monograph 6. Wellington: V. R. Ward, Government Printer.

Best, E. (1976). *Maori Religion and Mythology, Being an Account of the Cosmogony, Anthropogeny, Religious Beliefs and Rites, Magic and Folk Lore of the Maori Folk of New Zealand*, Part 1. Wellington: A. R. Shearer, Government Printer.

Best, E. (1982). *Maori Religion and Mythology, Being an Account of the Cosmogony, Anthropogeny, Religious Beliefs and Rites, Magic and Folk Lore of the Maori Folk of New Zealand*, Part 2. Wellington: P. D. Hasselberg, Government Printer.

Biard, J. (2001). The Natural Order in John Buridan, in J. M. M. H. Thijssen and J. Zupko, eds., *The Metaphysics and Natural Philosophy of John Buridan*. Medieval and Early Modern Science. Leiden: E. J. Brill, pp. 77–95.

Biggs, B. (1994). Knowledge as Allegory, in J. Morrison, P. Geraghty, and L. Crowl, eds., *Science of Pacific Island Peoples, Vol. 4: Education, Language, Patterns and Policy*. Suva, Fiji: Institute of Pacific Studies, pp. 1–11.

Bodde, D. (1991). *Chinese Thought, Society, and Science: The Intellectual and Social Background of Science and Technology in Pre-Modern China*. Honolulu, HI: University of Hawaii Press.

Boyd, R. (1993). Metaphor and Theory Change: What is "Metaphor" a Metaphor For?, in Andrew Ortony, ed., *Metaphor and Thought*, 2nd ed. Cambridge: Cambridge University Press, pp. 481–532.

Boyle, R. (1772). *The Works of the Honourable Robert Boyle*, ed. Thomas Birch. London: W. Johnston et al., vol. 1.

Boyle, R. (1996). *A Free Enquiry into the Vulgarly Received Notion of Nature* (1686), eds. E. B. Davis and M. Hunter. Cambridge Texts in the History of Philosophy. Cambridge: Cambridge University Press.

Brooke, J. H. (1991). *Science and Religion: Some Historical Perspectives*. The Cambridge History of Science Series. Cambridge: Cambridge University Press.

Bujard, M. (2009). State and Local Cults in Han Religion (2008), transl. J. Kieschnick and R. Llamas. In J. Lagerwey and M. Kalinowski, eds., *Early Chinese Religion – Part One: Shang through Han* (1250 BC–220 AD), vol. 2. Handbook of Oriental Studies 21: 1. Leiden: Brill, pp. 777–811.

Cadden, J. (1995). Science and Rhetoric in the Middle Ages: The Natural Philosophy of William of Conches. *Journal of the History of Ideas* 56(1), 1–24.

Calvin, J. (1961). *Institutes of the Christian Religion*, transl. F. Lewis Battles. Library of Christian Classics 20. London: SCM.

Ching, J. (1993). *Chinese Religions*. London: Macmillan Press.

Cunningham, A. and P. Williams (1993). De-centring the "Big Picture": The Origins of Modern Science and the Modern Origins of Science. *British Journal for the History of Science* 26(4), 407–32.

Curley, M. J. (1979) *The Physiologus*. Chicago, IL: University of Chicago Press.

Dawes, G. W. (2007) Can a Darwinian Be a Christian?, *Religion Compass* 1(6), 711–24.

Dawes, G. W. (2015). The Act of Faith: Aquinas and the Moderns, in Jonathan L. Kvanvig, ed., *Oxford Studies in Philosophy of Religion* 6. Oxford: Oxford University Press, pp. 58–86.

Dawes, G. W. (2016). *Galileo and the Conflict between Science and Religion*. Routledge Studies in the Philosophy of Religion. London: Routledge.

Dawes, G. W. (2017). Ancient and Medieval Empiricism, in E. N. Zalta, ed., *The Stanford Encyclopedia of Philosophy* (winter ed.). https://plato.stanford.edu/archives/win2017/entries/empiricism-ancient-medieval/.

Dawkins, R. (2006). *The God Delusion*, Boston, MA: Houghton-Mifflin.

De Cruz, H. (2018). Religion and Science, in E. N. Zalta, ed., *The Stanford Encyclopedia of Philosophy* (fall ed.). https://plato.stanford.edu/archives/fall2018/entries/religion-science/.

Denzinger, H. and A. Schönmetzer (1976). *Enchiridon Symbolorum Definitionum et Declarationum de Rebus Fidei et Morum*, 36th ed. Freiburg im Breisgau: Herder.

Descola, P. (2013). *Beyond Nature and Culture* (2005), transl. Janet Lloyd. Chicago, IL: University of Chicago Press.

Doar, B. (2010). Li Ling as a Postmillennial Chinese Intellectual. *Contemporary Chinese Thought* 42(1–2), 12–34.

Donald, M. (1991). *Origins of the Modern Mind: Three Stages in the Evolution of Culture and Cognition*. Cambridge, MA: Harvard University Press.

Donovan, A. (1996). *Antoine Lavoisier: Science, Administration and Revolution* (1993). Cambridge Science Biographies. Cambridge: Cambridge University Press.

Drake, S. (1980). *Galileo*. Past Masters. Oxford: Oxford University Press.

Draper, J. W. (1875). *History of the Conflict between Religion and Science*. International Scientific Series 12, New York: D. Appleton & Co.

Duhem, P. (1962). *The Aim and Structure of Physical Theory* 2nd ed. (1914), transl. Philip P. Wiener. New York: Atheneum.

Durkheim, É. (2010). Individual and Collective Representations (1898), in *Sociology and Philosophy*, transl. D. F. Pocock. Routledge Revivals. London: Routledge, pp. 1–15.

Eastwood, B. S. (1968). Medieval Empiricism: The Case of Grosseteste's Optics. *Speculum* 43 (2), 306–21.

Eno, R. (1990). *The Confucian Creation of Heaven: Philosophy and the Defense of Ritual Mastery*. SUNY Series in Chinese Philosophy and Culture. Albany, NY: State University of New York Press.

Evans-Pritchard, E. E. (1965). *Theories of Primitive Religion*. Oxford: Clarendon Press.

Evans-Pritchard, E. E. (1976). *Witchcraft, Oracles, and Magic among the Azande*, abridged by Eva Gillies. Oxford: Clarendon Press.

First, R. (1957). *We, the Tikopia: A Sociological Study of Kinship in Primitive Polynesia*. 2nd ed. London: George Allen & Unwin.

Firth, R. (1959). *Economics of the New Zealand Maori*. 2nd ed. Wellington: R. E. Owen, Government Printer.

Fung, Y.-L. (1953), *A History of Chinese Philosophy, vol. II: The Period of Classical Learning* (1934), transl. D. Bodde. Princeton, NJ: Princeton University Press.

Fung, Y.-M. (2009). Philosophy in the Han Dynasty, in Bo Mou, ed., *History of Chinese Philosophy*. Routledge History of World Philosophies 3. London: Routledge, pp. 269–302.

Galilei, G. (1960). The Assayer (1623), in S. Drake and C. D. O'Malley, eds., *The Controversy on the Comets of 1618*. Philadelphia, PA: University of Philadelphia Press, pp. 151–336.

Gaukroger, S. (2001). *Francis Bacon and the Transformation of Early-Modern Philosophy*. Cambridge: Cambridge University Press.

Genz, J. H. (2016). Resolving Ambivalence in Marshallese Navigation: Relearning, Reinterpreting, and Reviving the "Stick Chart" Wave Models. *Structure and Dynamics: eJournal of Anthropological & Related Sciences* 9 (1). https://escholarship.org/uc/item/43h1d0d7.

Genz, J. H. (2017). Without Precedent: Shifting Protocols in the Use of Rongelapese Navigational Knowledge. *Journal of the Polynesian Society* 126(2), 209–32.

Gethin, R. (1998). *The Foundations of Buddhism*. Opus Books. Oxford: Oxford University Press.

Gingras, Y. (2017). *Science and Religion: An Impossible Dialogue* (2016). Cambridge: Polity Press.

Gould, S. J. (2001). Nonoverlapping Magisteria, in Robert T. Pennock, ed., *Intelligent Design Creationism and Its Critics*. Cambridge, MA: MIT Press, pp. 737–49.

Graham, A. C. (1989). *Disputers of the Tao: Philosophical Argument in Ancient China*. La Salle, IL: Open Court.

Grant, E. (1974). *A Source Book in Medieval Science*. Source Books in the History of the Sciences. Cambridge, MA: Harvard University Press.

Gregory, T. (1966). L'idea di natura nella filosofia medievale prima dell'ingresso della fisica di Aristotele: Il secolo XII, in *La filosofia della natura nel Medioevo: Atti del terzo Congresso Internazionale di Filosofia medievale*. Milan: Società editrice Vita e pensiero, pp. 27–65.

Griffel, F. (2009). *Al-Ghazali's Philosophical Theology*. New York: Oxford University Press.

Grimble, A. (1972). *Migrations, Myth and Magic from the Gilbert Islands: Early Writings of Sir Arthur Grimble*, ed. R. Grimble. London: Routledge & Kegan Paul.

Haami, B. and M. Roberts (2002). Genealogy as Taxonomy. *International Social Science Journal* 54(173), 403–12.

Harper, D. (1990) The Conception of Illness in Early Chinese Medicine, as Documented in Newly Discovered 3rd and 2nd Century B.C. Manuscripts (Part I). *Sudhoffs Archiv* 74(2), 210–35.

Harper, D. (1999). Warring States Natural Philosophy and Occult Thought, in M. Loewe and E. Shaughnessy, eds., *The Cambridge History of Ancient China*. Cambridge: Cambridge University Press, pp. 813–84.

Harris, P. L. and M. Giménez (2005). Children's Acceptance of Conflicting Testimony: The Case of Death. *Journal of Cognition and Culture* 5(1), 143–64.

Harrison, P. (2015). *The Territories of Science and Religion*. Chicago, IL: University of Chicago Press.

Hervé, J. M. (1935). *Manuale theologiae dogmaticae* Paris: Berche et Pagis.

Hesse, M. (1988). The Cognitive Claims of Metaphor. *Journal of Speculative Philosophy NS* 2(1), 1–16.

Hinchman, L. P. and S. K. Hinchman (1991). Existentialism Politicized: Arendt's Debt to Jaspers. *Review of Politics* 53(3), 435–68.

Hobbes, T. (1998). *Leviathan*, ed. J. C. A. Gaskin. Oxford World's Classics. Oxford: Oxford University Press.

Hooykaas, R. (1972). *Religion and the Rise of Modern Science*. Edinburgh: Scottish Academic Press.

Huff, T. E. (1993). *The Rise of Early Modern Science: Islam, China, and the West*. Cambridge: Cambridge University Press.

Hume, D. (1978). *A Treatise of Human Nature*, ed. L. A. Selby-Biggie, 2nd ed. Oxford: Clarendon Press.

Hunn, E. (1982). The Utilitarian Factor in Folk Biological Classification. *American Anthropologist* 84(4), 830–47.

Husserl, E. (1970). *The Crisis of European Sciencs and Transcendental Phenomenology: An Introduction to Phenomenological Philosophy* (1954), trans. D. Carr. Northwestern University Studies in Phenomenology and Existential Philosophy. Evanston, IL: Northwestern University Press.

Hutchison, K. (1982). What Happened to Occult Qualities in the Scientific Revolution? *Isis* 73(2), 233–53.

Iacovetti, C. (2018). Filioque, Theosis, and Ecclesia: Augustine in Dialogue with Modern Orthodox Theology. *Modern Theology* 34(1), 70–81.

Jaeger, C. S. (1987). Cathedral Schools and Humanist Learning, 950–1150. *Deutsche Vierteljahrsschrift für Literaturwissenschaft und Geistesgeschichte* 61(4), 569–616.

John Paul II, Pope (1997). Message to the Pontifical Academy of Sciences. *Quarterly Review of Biology* 72(4), 381–3.

Johnston, I. (2010). *The Mozi: A Complete Translation*. Hong Kong: Chinese University Press.

Kahneman, D. and G. Klein (2009), Conditions for Intuitive Expertise: A Failure to Disagree. *American Psychologist* 64(6), 515–26.

Kaplan, David (2000). The Darker Side of the 'Original Affluent Society'. *Journal of Anthropological Research* 56(3), 301–24.

Kim, Y. S. (1982). Natural Knowledge in a Traditional Culture: Problems in the Study of the History of Chinese Science. *Minerva* 20(1–2), 83–104.

Kirschner, P. A. (1992). Epistemology, Practical Work and Academic Skills in Science Education. *Science & Education* 1(3), 273–99.

Klapproth, D. M. (2004). *Narrative as Social Practice: Anglo-Western and Australian Aboriginal Oral Traditions*. Language, Power, and Social Process 13. Berlin: Mouton de Gruyter.

Lang, H. S. (1989). Aristotelian Physics: Teleological Procedure in Aristotle, Thomas, and Buridan. *Review of Metaphysics* 42(3), 569–91.

Larson, E. (1997). *Summer for the Gods: The Scopes Trial and America's Continuing Debate Over Science and Religion*. New York: Basic Books.

Larson, E. (2003). *Trial and Error: The American Controversy Over Creation and Evolution*, 3rd ed. New York: Oxford University Press.

Lee, R. B. (1968). What Hunters Do for a Living, or, How to Make Out on Scarce Resources. In R. B. Lee and I. DeVore, eds., *Man the Hunter*. Chicago, IL: Aldine Publishing, pp. 30–48.

Leiss, W. (1974). *The Domination of Nature*. Boston, MA: Beacon Press.

Lennox, J. G. (2001). Aristotle on the Unity and Disunity of Science, *International Studies in the Philosophy of Science* 15(2), 133–44.

Lévy-Bruhl, L. (1926). *How Natives Think* (1910), transl. Lilian A. Clare. New York: Alfred A. Knopf.

Lévy-Bruhl, L. (1975). *The Notebooks on Primitive Mentality* (1949), transl. Peter Rivière. Explorations in Interpretative Sociology. New York: Harper & Row.

Lewis, D. (1994). *We, the Navigators: The Ancient Art of Landfinding in the Pacific*. 2nd ed. Honolulu: University of Hawaii Press.

Lindberg, D. C. (2007). *The Beginnings of Western Science: The European Scientific Tradition in Philosophical, Religious, and Institutional Context, 600 B.C. to A.D. 1450*. 2nd ed. Chicago, IL: University of Chicago Press.

Livingstone, D. N. (1997). *Darwin's Forgotten Defenders: The Encounter between Evangelical Theology and Evolutionary Thought* (1987). Vancouver: Regent College Publishing.

Livingstone, D. N. (2003). *Putting Science in its Place: Geographies of Scientific Knowledge*. Chicago, IL: University of Chicago Press.

Lloyd, G. E. R. (1968). *Aristotle: The Growth and Structure of His Thought*. Cambridge: Cambridge University Press.

Lloyd, G. E. R. (1999). Mythology: Reflections from a Chinese Perspective, in R. Buxton, ed., *From Myth to Reason? Studies in the Development of Greek Thought*. Oxford: Oxford University Press, pp. 145–67.

Lloyd, G. E. R. (2007). *Cognitive Variations: Reflections on the Unity and Diversity of the Human Mind*. Oxford: Clarendon Press.

Lloyd, G. E. R. and Nathan Sivin (2002). *The Way and the Word: Science and Medicine in Early China and Greece*. New Haven, CN: Yale University Press.

Locke, J. (1829). *An Essay Concerning Human Understanding*, 27th ed. London: Thomas Tegg.

Lohr, C. H. (1991). The Sixteenth-Century Transformation of the Aristotelian Division of the Speculative Sciences. In D. R. Kelly and R. H. Popkin, eds., *The Shapes of Knowledge from the Renaissance to the Enlightenment*. Archives Internationales d'Histoire des Idées/International Archives of the History of Ideas 123. Dordrecht: Springer, pp. 49–58.

Lovelock, J. (2000). *Gaia: A New Look at Life on Earth* (1979). Oxford: Oxford University Press.

Ludwig, D. (2018a). Revamping the Metaphysics of Ethnobiological Classification. *Current Anthropology* 59(4), 415–38.

Ludwig, D. (2018b). Letting Go of "Natural Kind": Toward a Multidimensional Framework of Nonarbitrary Classification. *Philosophy of Science* 85(1), 31–52.

Luhrmann, T. M. (1989). *Persuasions of the Witch's Craft: Ritual Magic in Contemporary England.* Cambridge, MA: Harvard University Press.

Luscombe, D. (2011). Crossing Philosophical Boundaries C. 1150–C. 1250. In S. E. Young, ed., *Crossing Boundaries at Medieval Universities.* Education and Society in the Middle Ages and the Renaissance 36. Leiden: Brill, pp. 7–27.

Maddock, K. (1970). Imagery and Social Structure at Two Dalabon Rock Art Sites. *Anthropological Forum* 2(4), 444–63.

Maddock, K. (1974). *The Australian Aborigines: A Portrait of their Society.* Harmondsworth: Penguin.

Major, J. S. (1993). *Heaven and Earth in Early Han Thought: Chapters Three, Four, and Five of the Huainanzi.* SUNY Studies in Chinese Philosophy and Culture. Albany, NY: State University of New York Press.

Malinowski, B. (2014). *Argonauts of the Western Pacific* (1922). Routledge Classics. London: Routledge.

Mbiti, J. S. (1969). *African Religions and Philosophy.* London: Heinemann Educational Books.

McRae, J. (2000). Maori Oral Tradition Meets the Book, in Penny Griffith, Peter Hughes, and Alan Loney, eds., *A Book in the Hand: Essay on the History of the Book in New Zealand.* Auckland: Auckland University Press, pp. 1–14.

McLaughlin, M. M. (1955). Paris Masters of the Thirteenth and Fourteenth Centuries and Ideas of Intellectual Freedom. *Church History: Studies in Christianity and Culture* 24(3), 195–211.

McMullin, E. (1998). Galileo on Science and Scripture, in P. Machamer, ed., *The Cambridge Companion to Galileo.* Cambridge: Cambridge University Press, pp. 271–347.

Merton, R. K. (1938). Science, Technology and Society in Seventeenth Century England. *Osiris* 4, 360–632.

Metzgar, E. H. (2008) Traditional Education in Micronesia: A Case Study of Lamotrek Atoll with Comparative Analysis of the Literature on the Trukic Continuum. PhD Thesis (1991), University of California, Los Angeles.

Moore, J. R. (1979). *The Post-Darwinian Controversies: A study of the Protestant struggle to come to terms with Darwin in Great Britain 1870–1900.* Cambridge: Cambridge University Press.

Murdoch, J. (1974). Philosophy and the Enterprise of Science in the Later Middle Ages. In Y. Elkana, ed., *The Interaction between Science and*

Philosophy. The Van Leer Jerusalem Foundation Series. Atlantic Highland, NJ: Humanities Press, pp. 51–74.

Needham, J. (1956). *Science and Civilization in China, vol. 2: History of Scientific Thought*. Cambridge: Cambridge University Press.

Norenzayan, A, (2013). *Big Gods: How Religion Transformed Cooperation and Conflict*. Princeton, NJ: Princeton University Press.

Norenzayan, A. (2015). Big Questions about Big Gods: Response and Discussion. *Religion, Brain & Behavior* 5(4), 327–39.

Numbers, R. L. (2006). *The Creationists: From Scientific Creationism to Intelligent Design*, exp. ed. Cambridge, MA: Harvard University Press.

Oresme, N. (1968). *Tractatus de configurationibus qualitatum et motuum*, in M. Clagett, ed., *Nicole Oresme and the Medieval Geometry of Qualities and Motions*. Madison, WI: University of Wisconsin Press.

Pankenier, D. W. (2013). *Astrology and Cosmology in Early China: Conforming Earth to Heaven*. Cambridge: Cambridge University Press.

Pasnau, R. (2015). Divine Illumination, in E. N. Zalta ed., *The Stanford Encyclopedia of Philosophy* (spring ed.). https://plato.stanford.edu/arch ives/spr2015/entries/illumination/.

Peacocke, A. (2001). *Paths from Science Towards God: The End of All Our Exploring*. Oxford: Oneworld.

Perkins, F. (2016). Metaphysics in Chinese Philosophy, in E. N. Zalta, ed., *The Stanford Encyclopedia of Philosophy* (winter d.). https://plato.stanford.edu /archives/win2016/entries/chinese-metaphysics/.

Peterson, W. J. (1980). "Chinese Scientific Philosophy" and Some Chinese Attitudes towards Knowledge about the Realm of Heaven-and-Earth. *Past & Present* 87, 20–30.

Plantinga, A. (2011). *Where the Conflict Really Lies: Science, Religion, and Naturalism*. New York: Oxford University Press.

Polanyi, M. (2009). *The Tacit Dimension* (1966). Chicago, IL: Chicago University Press.

Prytz-Johansen, J. (2012). *The Maori and His Religion in its Non-Ritualistic Aspects* (1954), new ed. Hau Classics of Ethnographic Theory 1. Manchester: *HAU, Journal of Ethnographic Theory*.

Pyssiäinen, I. (2003). True Fiction: Philosophy and Psychology of Religious Belief. *Philosophical Psychology* 16(1), 109–25.

Riedl, C. C. (1942). Introduction, in *Robert Grosseteste on Light (De Luce)*. Milwaukee, WI: Marquette University Press, pp. 1–9.

Roberts, J. H. (1988). *Darwinism and the Divine in America: Protestant Intellectuals and Organic Evolution, 1859–1900*. History of American Thought and Culture. Madison, WI: University of Wisconsin Press.

Ruse, M. (1997). John Paul II and Evolution. *Quarterly Review of Biology* 72(4), 391–5.

Ryle, G. (1946). Knowing How and Knowing That: The Presidential Address, *Proceedings of the Aristotelian Society*, NS 46, 1–16.

Sahlins, M. (1974). The Original Affluent Society, in *Stone Age Economics*. London: Tavistock Publications, pp. 1–39.

Sahlins, M. (2017). The Original Political Society. *Hau: Journal of Ethnographic Theory* 7(2),91–128.

Salmond, A. (2017). *Tears of Rangi: Experiments Across Worlds*. Auckland: Auckland University Press.

Schwartz, B. I. (1985). *The World of Thought in Ancient China*. Cambridge, MA: Belknap Press (Harvard University).

Sivin, N. (1995). The Myth of the Naturalists, in *Medicine, Philosophy and Religion in Ancient China: Researches and Reflections*. Variorum. Aldershot: Ashgate Publishing, chap. 4.

Smith, C. W. (2000). Straying Beyond the Boundaries of Belief: Maori Epistemologies Inside the Curriculum. *Educational Philosophy and Theory* 32(1), 43–51.

Smith, J. Z. (1972). I Am a Parrot (Red). *History of Religions* 11(4), 391–413.

Spelke, E. S. (1998). Nativism, Empiricism, and the Origins of Knowledge. *Infant Behavior and Development* 21(2), 181–200.

Sperber, D. (1975). *Rethinking Symbolism*, transl. A. L. Morton. Cambridge Studies in Social Anthropology 11. Cambridge: Cambridge University Press.

Sprat, T. (1734). *The History of the Royal Society of London for the Improving of Human Knowledge*. London: Printed for J. Knapton, et al.

Stanner, W. E. H. (1972). The Dreaming (1956). In W. A. Lessa and E. Z. Vogt, *Reader in Comparative Religion: An Anthropological Approach*, 3rd ed. New York: Harper & Row, pp. 269–77.

Stark, R. (2006). *The Victory of Reason: How Christianity Led to Freedom, Capitalism, and Western Success*. New York: Random House.

Stump, E. (1989). Faith and Goodness. *Royal Institute of Philosophy Lecture Series* 25, 167–91.

Suzman, J. (2017). *Affluence without Abundance: The Disappearing World of the Bushmen*. New York: Bloomsbury.

Swinburne, R. (2010). *Is There a God?*, rev. ed. Oxford: Oxford University Press.

Tambiah, S. J. (1985) *Culture, Thought, and Social Action: An Anthropological Perspective*. Cambridge, MA: MIT Press.

Tillyard, E. M. W. (1943). *The Elizabethan World Picture*. London: Chatto & Windus.

Tonkinson, R. (1978). Semen versus Spirit-Child in a Western Desert Culture. In L. R. Hiatt, ed., *Australian Aboriginal Concepts*. Canberra: Australian Institute of Aboriginal Studies/New Jersey: Humanities Press, pp. 81–92.

Tylor, E. B. (1913). *Primitive Culture*. 5th ed. vol. 2. London: John Murray.

Wach, J. (1947). *Sociology of Religion*. International Library of Sociology and Social Reconstruction. London: Kegan Paul, Trench, Trubner, & Co.

Wang, A. (2000). *Cosmology and Political Culture in Early China*. Cambridge Studies in Chinese History, Literature and Institutions. Cambridge: Cambridge University Press.

Wang, R. R. (2012). *Yinyang: The Way of Heaven and Earth in Chinese Thought and Culture*. New York: Cambridge University Press.

Watson, B. (2013). *The Complete Works of Zhuangzi*. New York: Columbia University Press.

Whitcomb, J. C. and H. M. Morris (1961). *The Genesis Flood: The Biblical Record and Its Scientific Implications*. Phillipsburg, NJ: Presbyterian and Reformed Publishing Company.

White, A. D. (1896). *A History of the Warfare of Science with Theology in Christendom*, 2 vols. London: Macmillan and Co.

Wilson, E. O. (2004). *On Human Nature*. Cambridge, MA: Harvard University Press.

Yang, C. K. (1961). *Religion in Chinese Society: A Study of Contemporary Social Functions of Religion and Some of Their Historical Factors*. Berkeley, CA: University of California Press.

Acknowledgments

My thanks to my colleagues John Shaver, who read an early version of this work and offered his comments as an anthropologist, and Brian Moloughney, who reassured me as I entered the world of Chinese thought, which I can know only at second-hand. My colleagues in the philosophy program have offered a wonderfully collegial environment in which to work. Last, but by no means least, my thanks are due to Kristin, *sine qua non*.

Cambridge Elements ≡

Philosophy of Religion

Yujin Nagasawa

University of Birmingham

Yujin Nagasawa is Professor of Philosophy and Co-Director of the John Hick Centre for Philosophy of Religion at the University of Birmingham. He is currently President of the British Society for the Philosophy of Religion. He is a member of the editorial board of *Religious Studies*, the *International Journal for Philosophy of Religion* and *Philosophy Compass*.

About the Series

This Cambridge Elements series provides concise and structured introductions to all the central topics in the philosophy of religion. It offers balanced, comprehensive coverage of multiple perspectives in the philosophy of religion. Contributors to the series are cutting-edge researchers who approach central issues in the philosophy of religion. Each provides a reliable resource for academic readers and develops new ideas and arguments from a unique viewpoint.

Cambridge Elements ≡

Philosophy of Religion

Printed in the United States
by Baker & Taylor Publisher Services